Teaching College Composition
A Practical Guide for New Instructors

Teaching College Composition

A Practical Guide for New Instructors

by
William Murdick

JAIN PUBLISHING COMPANY
Fremont, California

jainpub.com

Jain Publishing Company, Inc. is a diversified publisher of college textbooks and supplements, as well as professional and scholarly references, and books for the general reader. A complete, up-to-date listing of all the books, with cover images, descriptions, review excerpts, specifications and prices is always available on-line at **jainpub.com**.

Library of Congress Cataloging-in-Publication Data

Murdick, William.
  Teaching college composition : a practical guide for new instructors / by William Murdick.
      pages cm.
   ISBN 978-0-87573-104-9 (pbk. : alk. paper)
   1. English language–Rhetoric–Study and teaching. 2. English teachers–Training of. I. Title.
   PE1404.M867 2013
   808'.042071–dc23
                                              2013012861

Copyright © 2013 by William Murdick. All rights reserved. No part of this book may be reproduced, stored in a retrieval system, or transmitted, in any form or by any means, electronic, mechanical, photocopying, recording or otherwise, without the written permission of the publisher except for brief passages quoted in a review.

IMPORTANT—DON'T SKIP!

Style Issues

The writing expert Leo Rockas once equated being clear with being blunt. Bluntness also has the advantage of brevity. So I will be blunt in this booklet, even if it sometimes means being less than sweetly polite. Without sacrificing anything important, I want to keep the text as short as possible, something that can be read in a few days at most, since a new instructor may not have much time to get ready for Day One.

I will use the second person command point of view as often as possible. When the third person is unavoidable, I will avoid he/she entanglements by assuming that all composition instructors and college administrators are female, even though that is obviously not true. You guys will have to man up and be women for awhile. To be fair and balanced, when referring to students in the singular, I will use male pronouns.

Recommended Approach to Reading

Read Part I pretty much straight through, perhaps over the weekend before the term begins. There may be parts that you will want to review as the course proceeds, but have the whole thing under your belt, as a kind of overview, before you start teaching.

Part II discusses approaches to different assignments. Read sections in Part II as they become relevant to your course.

Note to Readers

Please take note of the purpose of the text, which is to get new teachers ready for Day One and provide them with a basic, usable, theory/research-based guide to best practices—but not the theory and research. That grounding will have to be acquired through one or more courses and lots of reading.

Contents

IMPORTANT—DON'T SKIP!   v

PART I: General Principles and Methods

1	Your Responsibilities	3
2	Course Syllabus	5
3	Textbooks	7
4	Copyright Laws	9
5	CYA	10
6	Sexual Harassment	11
7	Your Class Conduct	13
8	Their Class Conduct	14
9	Class Attendance	15
10	Technology	17
11	Support Services	19
12	Writing Centers	20
13	Sequencing Work	23
14	Writing Assignments	24
15	What Students Need to Know about Assignments	31
16	Putting Students in Groups	33
17	Pre-Writing Activities	37
18	Conducting Classroom Discussions	40

19	Critiquing Compositions: Quality and Tone	43
20	Critiquing Compositions: Your Major Concerns	45
21	Critiquing Compositions: Efficiency	51
22	Writing Conferences	53
23	Sentence Error: Politics and Pedagogy	55
24	Portfolio Assessment	60
25	Sample Portfolio Grading Sheet	66
26	Grading Individual Papers	69
27	Day One in Class	72
28	Evening One at Home	78
29	Day Two in Class	81

PART II: Teaching Six Types of Essay

30	The Five Paragraph Theme	87
31	The Personal Narrative Essay	97
32	The Informative Essay	101
33	The Argument on a Controversial Issue	108
34	The Literary Criticism Essay	116
35	The Long Research Paper	127

AFTERWORD: BECOMING A GREAT TEACHER   139

Part I

General Principles and Methods

1

Your Responsibilities

1-a To Yourself

Teaching composition is hard work, as you will soon find out. Above all, it is labor intensive, which is one reason why many tenured faculty don't like to teach it. At the end of the day there is often a stack of student essays awaiting your critique. If you are not willing to put in the hours to do a good job, you are in the wrong profession. Find something else that you can do with passion. Otherwise the grind will become unbearable, and the quality of your work will suffer.

You owe it to your students, your college, yourself, and your profession to put in the hours necessary to do a good job. One approach is to arrange course activities so that sets of papers are collected on Fridays. The weekend provides you with six units of time for review: Saturday morning, afternoon, and evening, and the same for Sunday. Do not try to handle more than two sets of papers in a single unit of time; one per unit is better. Divide the stack of papers into groups of six. Respond to a group and then get up and walk around, look out the window, get a cup of coffee. Give your brain a rest. Chapters 20-22 talk about how to actually critique the essays.

1-b To Your Students

As a composition teacher, you have three responsibilities to your students:

1. Provide them with useful work in the form of good writing assignments.
2. Guide them through a cycle of critique and revision.
3. Evaluate their work intelligently and fairly.

We will look at all three in detail later in this text, but that's your overview—the big picture. Keep it in mind as you read along.

You are not responsible for holding students' hands through their emotional crises, but you may want to, and there is nothing wrong with being sympathetic. Just don't get personally involved in their personal lives. Keep a distance. If you come across a serious problem, report it, don't try to fix it. Don't go to a coed's apartment and tell her boyfriend to stop beating her up.

1-c *To Your Department*

You also have a responsibility to your department, which is to follow the departmental syllabus. This is like your moral obligation to follow traffic laws, including the ones that don't make sense.

However, with departmental policy, you may be able to fudge. For example, if your department requires students to write only 5-paragraph themes (short thesis- and topic-sentence-controlled papers), and you would prefer to have your students produce more substantial pieces of writing, you might have them write a theme first, and then in the next assignment, have them expand it into a fuller essay. Or you might have them write themes the first half of the term and essays the second half. Talk to your composition director or department chair about this. With her permission, you can pay your obeisance to policy and then use your imagination to create a course more to your liking.

2

Course Syllabus

Your syllabus is your official description of the course. It carries the weight of a legal document in any dispute with a student about his grade and any questioning of your course requirements. Hand out your syllabus in printed form on the first day of class and post it online if you can. Put a copy on reserve in the library.

The syllabus should contain at least this information, roughly in this order:

- —your name along with your professional title (Ms., Mr., Professor, Dr.)
- —your office address and contact info; phone optional, e-mail necessary
- —the departmental description of the course, as it appears in the official catalogue of courses
- —required texts (you can recommend additional texts, but first-year students won't buy them; some won't even buy the required texts)
- —your grading and attendance policies
- —your classroom behavior policies
- —a summary of important work that students will be submitting, e.g., seven essays, 1 personal narrative, 1 informative or instructional, 1 response to a question about a reading, 4 persuasive in response to readings

—your week by week syllabus, showing how you are going to teach the course and providing tentative due dates for important work (you may not be able to do this for the first term that you teach; don't worry about it)

It is possible to devise a day-by-day syllabus, but you will find yourself having to change it frequently throughout the term. Too frequently. Even a weekly plan will have to be adjusted a number of times to allow for unforeseen disruptions, delays, or shifts in your plans.

3

Textbooks

If you are allowed to select your own textbook for the course, remember that almost all learning will come from the students' writing and then revising on the basis of critiques. Not from reading about writing, in other words. So don't ask your students to purchase a huge rhetoric at an astronomical price. You won't use most of the chapters and it's never worth the money.

You may, however, want to have your students purchase a small "reader," a book of essays. Such textbooks provide models of various kinds of essays. Your students would write their own essays inspired by, or in response to, the readings. These books are inevitably somewhat expensive, unless purchased used on the Internet. There are companies that will put together a small reader for you containing your selection of professional essays, obtaining the necessary permissions for you. (See, for example, the iDeal Reader/McGraw Hill.) The companies usually allow you to add text to the anthology, such as your syllabus or model student essays. That's something to look into once you have taught long enough to have a set of favorite published essays and a collection of good student work, with the student authors' permission to use their texts. The problem with the more traditional commercial readers is that they will contain many more essays than your students will read, and the students are paying the permissions cost and the printing cost for that unused content.

If you are looking for a rhetoric textbook, William Murdick's *A Student Guide to College Composition, 2nd Ed.*, discusses in depth the most difficult challenges of academic writing and shows students how to create a sophisticated first draft of various kinds of essays typically assigned in American colleges. It is inexpensive and can be used as a regular textbook, or students can use it on their own, independently of you. If seriously interested, ask for an examination e-copy at **jainpub.com**. Use the **Contact** link to make your request.

Do require the purchase of a compact handbook, like Diana Hacker's *A Pocket Style Manual*. Make it clear to your students that such a book will be useful all through college and beyond, so they shouldn't sell it at the end of the term.

It's very convenient if **all students have the same edition of the same handbook** so that, in your marginal comments on student papers, you can refer by page number or section number to passages in the book. This is something best handled at the department level so that students don't have to buy a new handbook for every composition course. You might lobby your department for a handbook requirement like Hacker's book if there isn't one already.

If faculty in your department are allowed to order their own textbooks, that clears the way for you to choose the handbook. However, sometimes even in that situation, a composition director will order books for adjunct faculty. If you are an adjunct, find out early on if the director will be ordering your books and ask her if you can choose a particular handbook or rhetoric or reader. She may go along with this because the main reasons for her ordering books for new instructors may not have anything to do with a desire to control their coursework, but instead may reflect the assumption that first-time instructors won't know much about composition textbooks and that they won't be on campus early enough to order texts that will be available at the beginning of the course.

If you choose the textbooks, stress the importance to your students of purchasing the correct edition (so that each student's text has the same page numbering). First-year college students don't know much about editions and won't consider the matter important unless you emphasize it.

4

Copyright Laws

Do not photocopy chapters or sections of books and distribute them to students without getting permission from the author or publisher, whoever owns the copyright. Take the trouble to contact the copyright owner (usually done through the publisher). Sometimes the fees are dirt cheap, though not always. In any case, don't put yourself or your college in jeopardy by breaking copyright laws.

Along the same lines, do not use student work without getting permission. Student writing is automatically copyrighted, like everyone else's written work. No copyright notice is required. You can ask students to give permission (in writing) to use their work in future classes, with or without their name attached, but do not harbor negative thoughts about those who refuse. Refusal is reasonable.

A student can legally make a single, personal-use copy of an article or essay you leave for him in the library, but such material cannot legally be used repeatedly from term to term, nor can it be used as a substitute for purchasing a textbook.

The *Chicago Manual of Style* offers a good primer on copyright law, if you are interested. Certain Web sites address Fair Use law, such as **https://www.xavier.edu/library/about/documents/Copyright 9-23-08.pdf**. An excellent government treatment of copyright law, worth printing for your files, can be found at

http://www.cendi.gov/publications/04-8copyright.html#toc20

5
CYA

CYA means Cover Your Anatomy, or protect yourself from the bureaucratic hammer coming down on your tiny fingers. Or your head.

Keep a CYA notebook and record at least these three types of information:

1. Commitments and promises made by you or others at meetings or over the phone. (Keep relevant e-mails.)
2. The exact words your dean or chair or composition director used to tell you to do something.
3. Clashes or uncomfortable encounters between you and administrators, faculty, or students.

Update your CYA notebook immediately after each encounter or meeting while the details and exact words are fresh in your mind. Begin each entry with date and location. Later, if you need to make a case to the higher ups, your credibility will soar if you produce "evidence" of the sort you have been keeping in your CYA notebook.

6

Sexual Harassment

It goes without saying, but it needs to be said anyway: keep your mitts off students. If something is burgeoning, delay any contact until the student is no longer taking one of your classes.

Most important: Find, read, and follow your school's sexual harassment policy. You may be surprised at how complex and restricting it is.

Certain basic rules apply regardless of the school policy:

— Always keep your office door half open when conferring with students.
— Never touch students. No congratulatory pats on the back or affectionate arm squeezes.
— Never make sexual jokes in class, especially ones directed at a particular student. You may think that you are dealing with a worldly group of adults, but you can be sure that somewhere among them is a student who is deeply offended by such non-professional remarks.

Harassment goes both ways. During every class you are the main object of attention, and some students are attracted to teachers, for whatever irrational reasons. Don't be surprised if a student calls you in the middle of the night expressing lewd thoughts. Or starts leaving little notes on your desk. Or even comes on to you face to face in your office or in class.

Ignore it with good humor as best you can. If the behavior continues, have a polite conversation with the student ("You are a charming person who shouldn't have trouble attracting appropriate people"). Don't be nasty. This is a human being with a human infatuation, not a monster. Probably. If the situation does get worrisome, report it to your boss, in writing and in person. In all such cases, even ones that *seem* innocent, keep detailed, dated entries in your CYA notebook. No interaction is completely innocent if it is personal.

7

Your Class Conduct

You can get away with wearing jeans and a sweatshirt to class, but it isn't smart. You are not a student and you shouldn't look like one. You are the authority in the classroom, the one responsible for making things work, and you should look like the big Kahuna. Pukui and Elbert's *Hawaiian Dictionary* defines *Kahuna* as a "Priest, sorcerer, magician, wizard, minister, expert in any profession." That's you. Dress up for it. You will get more respect from your students, which is very useful. The last thing you want in your composition class is a discipline problem (i.e., high school tomfoolery).

Always be courteous and respectful, no matter how frustrated or angry you are. That's part of your job—you are the voice of reason. The same voice you are trying to teach students to use in their writing. Say "please" and "thank you" as a matter of routine.

Don't talk down to students. Especially don't use sarcasm to put students down or belittle their ideas. Students hate sarcasm directed at them, and rightfully so.

8

Their Class Conduct

You have to have rules for classroom behavior, and not just because some of your students will be kids away from home for the first time. You will inevitably experience inappropriate behavior from older students as well.

You can invent any sensible rule you want, but below are some that should probably be on your list. Don't hide them from the students. Make sure your students get this list on the first day of class. Put it in your syllabus that you hand out on Day One and, if possible, put it online where they can access it.

- —No talking to a neighbor when the instructor or another student is addressing the class
- —No cellular devices can be used to receive or send messages during class
- —No hats
- —No eating in class
- —No sleeping in class
- —No working on assignments due at the beginning of the class or on assignments for other classes
- —No late arrivals or early departures. See your instructor after class to explain lateness. See your instructor in advance to explain a need to leave early.

You might give a quiz on these rules on the second class meeting. Nothing focuses a student's mind more than an impending quiz.

9

Class Attendance

Inform your students that regular class attendance is required for passing this course and that cutting class is the single most common reason for failure in college courses, including composition classes. Truer words cannot be spoken.

If you follow this book's advice and use portfolio assessment (see Chapter 24), you will not need to take attendance. If you don't use portfolio assessment, but you follow this book's advice and have students sit and work in groups (see Chapter 16), you can take attendance in a few seconds by eyeballing each group and noticing who is missing. Otherwise, you will have to go through the list of students enrolled in the course looking for their faces in the crowd or calling out their names. But do it.

Eventually you are going to encounter a student who writes well and turns in all the essays and gets good grades on them, but cuts a lot of classes. Such students, if given less than an A or B in the course because of penalties for absences, may go to your department chair or the college dean and complain about your attendance policy. You had better be prepared to defend that policy.

Make sure your attendance policy is published in the course syllabus, with a full explanation as to why. Below are two justifications you might use, and you have my permission to copy them word for word, if you wish, without giving me credit:

—In this course, learning is a collaborative effort in which students help each other with critiques and learn to develop a critical eye from doing so. A student who misses many classes obviously cannot participate in this helping and learning experience.

—The course teaches aspects of writing (such as a sophisticated writing process, rhetorical information, and editing techniques) that effect long term development, and that kind of learning can only be acquired by being in class. A student, therefore, cannot earn a good grade simply by starting with a competent grade-level writing ability and then turning in the assigned essays. If that were the case, then such students would be exempted from the course in the first place.

If things aren't going your way in a grade dispute, you can make an offer of compromise with the administrator and the student. Assuming that your college offers a PASS/FAIL grading option, here's a respectable offer: Instead of giving the student a poor grade, you will go along with giving him no-grade credit for the course, which would go down on the student's record as a PASS.

Stick up for yourself and your profession—teachers grade students, students don't determine their own grades, and that's an important principle. But don't become obnoxious or fiercely stubborn about it. Getting rehired next term is more important than any student's grade. Know when to fold 'em.

10

Technology

10-a Computer Skills

Require computer skills, but don't teach them. That's not your job. There should be computer lab workers for that. For word processing, provide your students with a list of functions they will need in order to do college work. Besides the fundamentals, students will find the following functions useful if not necessary:

> Save As; line spacing; font size and style; margins; headers and footers, including page numbering; text centering; regular indentation for long quotations and hanging indentation for bibliographies; find; find and replace; spell check, dictionary, and thesaurus.

10-b Online Sites for Classes

Local area network (**LAN**) sites or Web sites for individual classes allow you to post assignments and other course work, collect student work, post student writings for peer commentary, and keep your grades, among other things. If the school's computer facilities allow it, establish a **LAN** site for each class. If you don't know how to do that, consult the network gurus. Alternatively, you can establish a Web site for your classes. Be mindful of the need for privacy. Again, technical help should be available on campus.

This may be something you will want to delay until you get comfortable teaching composition, but if you are in the business for the long run, establishing network sites for your classes is worth doing. Don't be hesitant because of your own ignorance about networks and Web sites. Get help and learn.

At the very least, establish a non-interactive Web site where you can leave information about classes. Students may sometimes query you via e-mail. Your college will provide you with an e-mail address for your professional work.

11

Support Services

Your institution undoubtedly offers support services for handicapped and learning disabled students, and some of those services may be relevant to composition. For instance, a visually impaired student may have trouble using computers in the labs, but the support services folks may have a large screen computer for them to use. Or a non-ambulatory student may not be able to access a computer lab on the second floor of a building, in which case the services lab, which will be accessible, may be able to supply the software and, with your assistance, other files you use for your course. Learning disabled students are sometimes offered assistance in proofreading. Know the ins and outs of support services. Pay those folks a visit and have a friendly chat. Ask them what they do for composition students.

Your school's writing center is probably the most important support service for composition. See the next chapter.

12

Writing Centers

Writing centers exist to help composition students and others, sometimes even faculty, with their writings. You can assign students to take a draft of their paper to the writing center for a critique. Require that they get the tutor to sign the draft to validate the visit if you are giving points for such visits towards the student's grade. This use of the writing center is consistent with the essential truth about teaching writing: That students learn mainly by being coached through a cycle of critique and revision.

Writing Centers are usually manned by English graduate students or undergraduate English majors, though sometimes a tenured English faculty member will be assigned limited duty there, most likely to fill out her schedule when one of her courses didn't run. Nowadays, writing centers are often directed by a faculty member trained in composition theory. But don't depend on it. Ask around about the credentials of your writing center's director. The more you know about a service you are using, the better.

Writing centers can play an important role in helping you fulfill your goal of improving student writing. But be aware of potential problems. When Writing Centers first appeared on the scene in the 1970s, many English faculty believed that getting writing center help would constitute cheating. Some still do. The problem with that reasoning is that it prioritizes grading over learning. As a teacher, you have an administrative duty to grade, but your main obligation is to teach, and everything else is secondary. A well-run writing center is a teaching station.

12. Writing Centers

Sometimes writing center tutors do indeed take over a student's paper and write at least some of it for him. The student learns very little from that experience. A sophisticated, competent writing center director will train her tutors to help a student without taking away ownership of the paper. Even so, some of that training may not work for some of the tutors. It is up to you to keep an eye on what is happening with your students when they go to the writing center. When you examine your students' drafts which they took to the writing center, look for evidence of the tutor writing on the paper—cross outs, word changes, new sentences—done with a different handwriting or color ink than the student is using to make his own changes on the printed copy. It's not hard to detect such intervention from a tutor.

Besides you, no one should make corrections on a student's paper except the student author himself. For example, if a writing center tutor notices a misspelled homophone such as *its* for *it's* and points it out, the student author should be the one who takes out a pen and changes it. This added kinesthetic element to correction enhances learning. When the writer physically and mentally spells the word correctly himself, using eye, hand, and verbal brain activity, he is more likely to remember and learn. This goes for grammatical corrections as well.

If you are having trouble with writing center tutors writing on your students' papers, schedule an informal chat with the director. Don't accuse specific tutors. You are not there to get anyone in trouble, but to solve a problem. Do not talk to the tutors yourself; that would amount to stepping on the toes of the director and may produce an unpleasant reaction.

Almost any writing center director will be happy to cooperate with a composition instructor's reasonable requests. You might ask that tutors, after reading your students' drafts, respond by using the kind of controlled response sheet shown in Figure 1 in Chapter 16, which your student would bring to the writing center stapled to his paper. In other words, the tutor would respond to evaluation questions that you devised and would point to places in the essay where problems occur. The tutor might also orally confer with the student about how such problems will get solved.

Cheap wooden chop sticks make good pointers for group members critiquing each other's papers and for writing center tutors. You might pass them out to your students and tell them to use them in class and bring with them when they visit the writing center.

For a regular Composition I course, a student might get a critique from (1) his fellow students in class, (2) from a writing center tutor, and (3) from you, and would revise after each critique. The final copy would be the fourth draft. You will find, however, that some students visit the writing center more often than required. Some in fact become enamored of the place and hang out there, eating a bag lunch with the tutors, getting to know them personally, and routinely getting advice from the ones they like. They may well continue this relationship beyond your class, possibly for the rest of their college career. There is nothing wrong with this. In fact, these students will likely progress more than their peers. Even if they started out weak, on graduation day writing center devotees will often be among the best writers your college sends out into the workplace.

13

Sequencing Work

The most common sequence of composition courses in the U.S. consists of three courses: a basic course for weak writers, a regular essay-writing course, and a second essay writing course that includes a long research paper. Many variations on the composition program exist, however, and you would be wise to get a good understanding of the sequence within which your course or courses reside.

As students progress through a sequence, they will be asked to write more difficult essays. Essays become more difficult to write when they are longer and require the juggling of more outside sources. Thus a student may first be asked to write a 2-3 page narrative essay or informative article based on his own experience alone; then an essay of that same length in response to a single essay in the required textbook; then a 3-5 page essay in response to several sources, some of which he finds in the library. In the final assignment in a multi-course sequence, he may be asked to juggle ten or twelve voices besides his own in the writing of a 10-12 page research paper.

Your own writing assignments should reflect an understanding of this sequencing of work. The next section discusses assignments in detail.

14

Writing Assignments

Your department may require certain types of assignments. Assuming, however, that you have some latitude, this section will help you decide what kinds of essays you will ask your students to write. Part II gives detailed advice about how to teach different types of essay, including more suggestions about assignments.

14-a Personal Narrative Essays

Over the last forty years or so, the issue of what kinds of writing first-year composition students should do has been a subject of great debate. Early proponents of "expressive writing" have made the point that students should write about things they know about, and since they are not yet experts in anything, the subjects they know most thoroughly are their own personal experiences. Therefore, they should write about those personal experiences, expressing their feelings and thoughts.

Actually, it's not true that students have no expertise in anything, but we can leave that part of the argument alone for now. By writing personal narrative essays, students can learn a lot about how to think deeply about a subject through the act of writing, as well as how to educate readers. In Chapter 31, you will find a discussion of how to teach this kind of composition.

In a typical narrative essay, a student will recount an experience which taught him something about himself or some other person.

14-b *Personal Knowledge Essays*

Another type of writing assignment that comes from personal experience is one in which the student teaches the reader something the student knows about. See Chapter 32 for advice on how to teach this essay.

You will have to help some students find suitable topics drawing on their expertise, because their first reaction will be that they don't know anything worth writing about. That's never true. A student says to you: "I never did anything because I had to stay home all the time after school and on weekends taking care of my baby brother so my mother could work." You say to him: "You know enough about taking care of infants to write a book on the subject." Then you help him reduce his subject to something focused enough for a three-page composition.

Ask your students to consider work and school experience to find topics to write on. Students can also write about things they are interested in but don't yet know about, in which case they will have to begin by doing some research. As an instructor, don't take the attitude that research and documentation of sources are something for a later course. It's never too early to start learning how to research and write from sources and how to document those sources, and students can handle that even in "remedial" courses.

Inform your students that the best writers are passionate about their subjects, and they take the trouble to become experts. Students shouldn't hesitate to research even those topics they already know a lot about. They should take the attitude that all papers are research papers, even a short, single-paragraph mini-essay. If you expect them to, your students will make writing-from-research their standard approach to writing, and that will serve them far beyond their composition courses.

14-c *Professional Work Essays*

At various times in the past few decades, some composition theorists have concluded that students should start learning how to write the kinds of texts they will have to produce for their professional work. There are a number of problems with this approach, not the least of which is that composition instructors don't know much about the rhetoric of empirical reports in biology, marketing publications, client reports in psychology, etc., so how are they going to teach those types of prose? Preparing students for writing in the professional world is something that individual departments must take on, introducing their own upperclassmen to these genres.

Nevertheless, you can encourage students to research and write on subjects connected to their majors and their career ambitions. Ask a physics major to explain the physics of global warming, or a history major to contemplate the lessons we can draw from the battle at Thermopylae, or an art major to contrast the Baroque and Rococo styles of painting.

14-d *Academic Essays*

Probably the most commonly-held belief today among composition experts is that composition programs, courses, and assignments should be teaching students mainly how to do the kind of writing they will do in college. For one thing, this justifies the college's requiring a series of composition courses as part of General Education. Academic writing here means writing in response to reading, that is, writing texts in which students analyze information and opinions, summarize them, and respond to them with a critical eye, sometimes using formal methods of argumentation.

14. Writing Assignments

Most composition instructors use a reader for this kind of course, often one that contains essays that take a position on contemporary controversial issues. Reading and writing these kinds of essays has the additional advantage of teaching students about what is going on in the adult world. Many 18-year-old freshmen don't even read a newspaper; few could tell you the basic arguments that have been put forth in defense of, or in opposition to, abortion or gun control or gay marriage, just to name a few hot topics today. A textbook like *Current Issues and Enduring Questions* (Barnes & Noble) introduces students to philosophical controversies that have been raging for thousands of years, as well as new ones appearing on today's editorial pages.

Below are eight examples of assignments based on reading:

(1) You can pose a penetrating question about an essay the students have read and discussed in class. For example, after discussion of Martin Luther King's "I Have a Dream" speech, you can ask students to write on whether or not Dr. King's dream has come true, and why or why not.

(2) You can use essays as points of departure or inspiration. Using the King speech again as an example, you could ask your students to write their own "Dream" speech about some specific aspect of life in America.

(3) The most straightforward kind of writing assignment in the academic category is to ask students to take a side on a controversial issue, let's say whether or not private ownership of hand guns should be banned in the U.S. This is assuming your textbook reader has for-and-against essays on the issue.

Besides the textbook, your students should be using the library and the Web to find additional sources. However, early in the term, you might restrict class discussion (see Chapter 18) and essay reading to the writings that appear in the reader. This is a good safe environment for your first lessons on citation and bibliography. The students will be dealing with only a few essays, all of the same type—an article in a collection.

(4) Much argumentation can be analyzed as problem-solution rhetoric. Ask your students to write an essay that answers questions like these about an essay they have just read and discussed: What problem or problems is this essay addressing? Are the problems real? Are they important? Has the author missed a more important problem related to the issue under discussion? Is the author using questionable premises or lines of reasoning? What are the author's solutions? Will they work? Do the writer's solutions produce bad effects and do those outweigh the good effects? Are there better solutions?

(5) As Chapter 33 points out, you can also ask students to write a compromise argument, bringing together two divergent views into one that takes into account the desires of both groups. This requires an understanding and analysis of both sides and a creative solution.

(6) You may be assigned, or volunteer for, a section of composition for a particular major. Here's an example from the University of Pittsburgh that would work for primary and secondary education majors.

> **ENGCMP 0207 Seminar in Composition: Education**
> This version of Seminars in Composition includes readings that consider issues of teaching and learning in American education, and for this reason may be of special interest to students who plan to become

teachers. All sections will require at least one crafted composition per week as well as participation in class discussion about writing and education.

In this case, you will have to do some research yourself to find out what the major (perhaps controversial) issues are within a profession, in order to come up with stimulating assignments.

(7) You might arrange to team teach a first-year course with an instructor in another field, such as psychology. Students would take the intro course in psychology from your partner and a special section of composition for psychology majors from you. In this case, you might require a textbook like Roger Hock's *Forty Studies That Changed Psychology* and then assign students to read and respond to important experiments, such as Stanley Milgram's study of obedience to authority.

(8) Want to go high tech? Though it may not be practical for you at the outset of your teaching career, an interesting approach to assignments is to assign Web sites, instead of essays. Each web site would contain a traditional essay expanded by links, some to visuals, some to other writers' critical work, and some to additional work by the student. Students would work on their sites all semester long (and possibly beyond that).

Since their work is "published" and open to the world, students inevitably take a keen interest in seeing to it that they don't make fools of themselves with shallow treatments of subjects and with mechanical errors. Consider the passage below from an article in the online *Washington Post* ("Wikipedia Goes to Class," May 30, 2011). Professors around the country, at the encouragement of Wikipedia, had recently begun asking students to write Wikipedia articles, which would be open to change and even the heartless criticism of Wiki editors and anonymous readers. The *Post* comments:

> Rochelle A. Davis, an assistant professor at Georgetown University, told undergraduates in her culture and politics course to create a Wikipedia page about a community they belonged to, then use that research to develop a thesis for an academic paper. "Collectively, they were the best papers I've ever read at Georgetown," Davis said. She said students benefited from vetting their ideas with a wider community. . . .

For a Web site course, you might arrange a team-taught pair of courses in composition and Web publishing, the latter taught by a computer science instructor.

15

What Students Need to Know about Assignments

For each assignment, provide your students with as much of the following as possible, as soon as possible:

1. Due dates for rough drafts and the final version

2. The length and format requirements (for example, 800-1,000 words, double-spaced text)

3. The type of essay (for example, a "personal narrative" or an "argument on a controversial issue"); a standard designation of essay type will be useful when students go to the writing center. If students are using a textbook like Murdick's *A Student Guide to College Composition*, 2nd *Ed.*, it will help them turn to the appropriate section in that book for help

4. The learning goals, including any specific in-class learning that is supposed to be evident in the essay (such as proper form for quotations or proper use of the apostrophe)

5. Any organizational requirement (for example, a formal introduction and conclusion; or a point-by-point comparison)

6. Any content requirement (for example, information from an online source; or at least one quotation)

7. Any specified audience, or imagined reader, other than the instructor

8. The criteria for grading. If you are not grading holistically and you have created an evaluation scale showing the relative weight given to sentence correctness, appropriate style, content development, use of outside sources, and other features, distribute this scale at the outset before students begin to write. You will almost certainly want to create an analytical grading sheet for the long research paper

9. A model essay and how that essay fulfills the assignment. You can write such essays yourself, but it is better to use real ones from your own students, accumulated as time goes by. For each student essay, make sure you have the writer's permission to use it as a model. Keep written permissions in a file along with copies of the essays.

Note: You should have a group e-mail file for each composition class (a single file name that sends e-mail messages to the whole class). One way to distribute model essays, as well as other material, is to send them out to the class as e-mail attachments. That saves the cost of reproducing them through printing, it allows you to distribute material before the next class, it ensures that students who are absent get the material, and it reduces the possibility of a student losing it (if he mistakenly erases it, he can have a group member e-mail him another copy).

16

Putting Students in Groups

Peers are great teachers, and collaborative activities can lead to significant learning. That's what the research says, and that's what you'll find out once you start using collaborative work as part of your teaching.

Put your students into groups of four or five people. That should mean no more than six groups maximum, ideally five. These groups will work together in class, and perhaps sometimes out of class, for the whole term. There are other ways of arranging collaborative learning in a composition classroom, such as rotating group membership or establishing writing partners, but permanent small groups of this sort work well for a number of writing and discussion activities. No special teaching skills are required on your part.

Wait until you have initial writing samples before forming groups. You don't want all weak writers in one group. Mix up men and women. They will have to work with each other in the professional workplace, so they might as well start getting used to it.

16-a Group Leaders

Assign a group leader for the day. You can do that on a rotation basis, so that each student takes on that role regularly. Or you can have fun with it, announcing that the group leader today will be the person with the most space between the eyes or the person with the most comfortable shoes or the person with the biggest head of hair. Let the students joke around with that for a minute. It loosens them up and wakes them up, gets them talking, gets them ready for active learning.

The group leader (1) keeps group members on task, and (2) reports group ideas to the whole class. Explain those roles, because they won't know until you tell them.

16-b Idea Generation

Use groups for idea generation. Let's say your students have just read Michael Levin's often anthologized essay "The Case for Torture." Before asking them to write on this subject, you want to make sure that they consider the case *against* torture. You might ask students to think up and write down one or two reasons why Levin may be wrong. Next, ask them to get into their groups and share those ideas with the rest of the group. Then have group leaders share those collections of ideas with the whole class. You act as secretary and create a master list on the blackboard.

16-c Critiquing Drafts

Use groups for critiquing drafts. The students won't really know how to do this at first on their own, so provide them with guidance. A simple response sheet, which you can vary according to the nature of the assigned essay, is sufficient to provide important feedback before revision. Figure 1 provides an example that could be used for an essay in response to Michael Levin's essay "The Case for Torture."

If a student, for example, in the course of reading a fellow group member's draft essay, found a line of reasoning that didn't make sense to him, he would put a **2** in the margin next to that problem and perhaps parentheses around the

Figure 1: Model Critique Sheet for Levin Essay

1 = Yes   2 = Somewhat   3 = No

___ **Essay does what the teacher asked for**

___ **Levin's view is presented completely and fairly**

___ **Essay maintains a mature tone**

Point To's (put number in the margin of the essay)

1. **Awkward spots that need rephrasing**
2. **Places where the meaning or logic is unclear**
3. **Sections that could be developed more**
4. **Sections that don't seem to belong in the essay or that seem to be out of place**
5. **Word errors or sentence errors**

---

offending passage. At the end of the review, the student reader would put his initials on the critique sheet and next to numbers in the margin. That way the student writer knows who to query about a criticism if he doesn't understand it. During within-group discussions after the critiques, students can expand on the critique sheet by giving suggestions on solving problems. While all this is going on, you tour the classroom, helping to keep the groups on task and offering your opinions when asked.

You can invent individual Critique Sheets for each writing assignment, though you might keep the first question (Does what the teacher asked for) and the Point To's the same for every writing assignment.

Depending on how much time you have allotted for this group activity and how long the drafts are, a student would normally leave the class with two or three critiques of his draft and a number of ideas as to how to improve his paper with a revision. Of course, the student can decline to follow these suggestions if he doesn't like them. But if two or three of his fellow students put the same **Point To** number in the same place, that might be persuasive.

Talk to your class about how writers should view criticism, about how to give it and how to receive it. (You give it in as nice a tone as possible, and you receive it in as grateful a mood as you can muster.) You might note that professional writers seek out criticism from loved ones and friends. And when their work has been accepted by a publisher, an editor will often suggest, or even insist on, changes. It is all part of the collaborative nature of most writing.

17

Pre-Writing Activities

Explain to your students that professional writers rarely approach the blank page with a blank mind. They have thought about their subject and may have undertaken research, note taking, outlining, conversations, and other pre-writing activities designed to get the project underway, at least mentally, ahead of composing the first draft.

Get your students engaged in similar pre-writing activities as they begin thinking about their first essay. Below are some suggestions you can make and some activities you can activate.

17-a Talk to Yourself

Suggest to your class: "While walking across campus or while working out in the gym or while commuting to campus, day dream and talk to yourself about your paper. Imagine a reader and talk to that invisible person, sharing your ideas, your questions, your emotions."

Now, having passed on that idea, tell your students to take out a piece of paper and a writing instrument and write down two occasions today and tomorrow when they can do this in a practical way. Call on students to share their plans with the class. This kind of sharing gives ideas to other students.

17-b Talk to a Real Person

You say to the class: "Explain to your roommate, your friend, your sweetie, your sibling, your parent that you are writing a paper on such and such a topic. What do they think about the subject? What would they want to learn about it from your paper? Most people will be flattered that you would be interested in their opinion and will offer it freely."

Now, have students write down the names of two people they can talk to about their work. Ask around the class—who can you talk to about your essay?

17–c Talk on Paper

Have your students start generating ideas on paper in class by writing phrases and sentences. Teach them free writing: "Free writing is a technique in which you write about your subject as fast as you can, letting your unconscious mind emit a flow of words. If you hit a brick wall, keep repeating the last five or six words until something new pops up."

Five minutes of free writing usually results in some ideas that the writer can work with to start designing an essay.

17-d Create a Faux Outline or List

Not the formal type of outline with Roman numerals and capital letters, just a list of phases or sentences. Tell your students to list three main ideas that their paper will look at. Then tell them to take each of those and write down two or three things they will say about each part of the paper. This won't necessarily be their final outline or the final structure to their essay. It is simply a way of thinking about the subject. Professional writers will often take the easiest part that they have imagined this way and begin composing it. This gets them going on the actual writing.

17. Pre-Writing Activities

17-e Map Ideas

Teach your students how to plan by mapping. Create on the blackboard for them a sample idea map with words inside circles and lines connecting them in ways that show the connections between ideas. In the middle, there should be a big circle with, perhaps, the title. All the other circles spring from it.

A fairly big circle with an idea or topic inside it might have several little circles extending out from it with key words or phrases inside those little circles, and some smaller circles popping out of them with words or phrases in them.

Imagine that you are writing a similar assignment yourself. For your model, create an idea map that would work for you. You can then put that on the blackboard as an example.

17-f Plan and Do Research

Say to your students: "Figure out what you will need to learn about your topic and then go start reading or interviewing people or observing/testing phenomena, whatever kind of research you need to do. As you learn about your topic, ideas will begin to occur to you as to what you want to say in your essay."

Now, ask students to write down two things they will need to learn before completing their paper. Have some students share what they have written down.

18

Conducting Classroom Discussions

The less you talk in the classroom and the more the students talk, the better. As the writing sage Donald Murray used to point out: The students are there to learn to think and express ideas in language—you've already acquired those abilities.

So don't hog the language microphone.

18-a Generating Talk

Come into class with a prepared set of provocative questions, ones that will draw out useful information, analysis, and ideas that will help your students in their writing assignment.

Students in large numbers will willingly talk about an issue if they have thought about it. Otherwise they usually sit in silence, waiting for you to answer your own questions. Writing is a form of thinking. At the opening of class discussion, for example, you might tell students to get out paper and a writing instrument and write on this question: What was the most important point that Martin Luther King made in his "I Have a Dream" speech and why do you think so? Give them five minutes. Now ask the same question for oral response, and hands will go up.

Always give students a chance to answer your questions. Don't ask questions and then, after ten seconds, answer them yourself. They'll get used to that and expect it and will rarely bother to break the pattern. A long wait will almost always yield an answer from someone. Be patient.

18. Conducting Classroom Discussions

On the other hand, don't wait forever. You have to keep things moving. (You can see why teaching is sometimes called an art.) If nobody says anything for a long time, you can say, "Ok, nothing is clicking. That's OK. Take out a piece of paper and a writing instrument. [Pause while they do that.] You have one minute to answer, in writing, the question I just raised. These will be collected. The person who writes the most, staying on subject, gets a free doughnut next class. Go!" After they write for one minute, put the students in their groups and ask them to come to some conclusions on the issue, and then call on group leaders to report.

Collect those pieces of writing. This gives students point credit for having been in class today to do this in-class exercise in writing-to-learn (WTL).

Don't forget to bring the donut to the next class, in a plastic zip-lock bag. Your word is a sacred trust.

18-b Purposes of Discussions

Discussions should have a purpose. Discussion of an essay should serve the purpose of providing ideas and inspiration for a writing assignment. You are not being paid by the tax payers and tuition payers to teach students about your views on some political or social issue separate from the writing your students are doing. Yes, it's OK to demonstrate once or twice what brilliant intellectualism sounds like, but do it within the context of your students' development of a particular essay. Teachers who regularly take up class time sounding off on their political or religious or philosophical views soon get a reputation for doing that, and they lose respect among students, other faculty, and administrators.

18-c Individual to Group to Whole Class to Individual

Ask students to write for three minutes on a question, then share their ideas with fellow group members. Then ask group leaders to start off a whole class discussion based on what their group members have been saying, including their own views.

During classroom discussions, you are the class recorder. As students come up with ideas, you put them on the blackboard. When that's done, everyone contemplates the whole of the class's creative thinking. Individuals take what they want from the bounty on the blackboard for their own use in writing their essay.

Make this your typical in-class sequence: Individual to Group to Whole Class to Individual.

19

Critiquing Compositions: Quality and Tone

Most of your work outside of class will consist of responding to student writing. This is something you must become good at. It is the heart of your teaching, the point where you touch and teach your students individually. You will note as you read the three chapters on this subject that "teaching" often means setting the student on a path to learning, rather than telling him how to fix something.

19-a Use Your Computer

Some teachers, like students, have sloppy handwriting. Teacher comments that are unreadable are worse than useless—they frustrate and infuriate students. If your handwriting is poor, learn to print fast.

Or better yet, follow this method. Read papers next to your computer and write your comments with your word processor. Number each typed comment and use a colored pen to number the appropriate spot in the essay where the comment applies. Print your comments and staple them to the student's text. There are obviously no problems of unreadable handwriting with this approach. Just as important, you will be able to say more and edit your comments to improve them. This approach takes only slightly longer and produces much higher quality response.

19-b Be Careful about Tone

Don't ever forget that every negative remark you make about someone's writing hurts that person to the bone. This doesn't mean that you shouldn't ever make such criticisms. Just keep in mind their emotional effect. A lot of negativity turns some students off to writing in general. They decide, wrongly, that they "just can't write." When that happens, you have failed as a teacher.

Many of the traditional comments found on student essays are meaningful only to the instructor. They are too vague to be comprehensible and useful to a student unfamiliar with the rhetorical ideas underlying the shorthand of English-teacher-talk. Here are some examples of the kind of useless, tone deaf prose you should avoid:

—Doesn't make sense
—You're missing the point of the Copperud essay
—Don't do this
—Too shallow
—I don't get it—what are you saying?
—Confusing
—You're contradicting yourself
—Essay is underdeveloped

In your critiques of work-in-progress, the focus should be on how to improve the text in the next draft, not the poor quality of this one. Suggest how the paper can be strengthened. More "you might do this" than "this is bad."

Explain why some part of the text is deficient; don't just state that it is. If there is a contradiction, explain the contradiction. If you are confused, offer alternative understandings to show why a reader might not be sure of the meaning of the text. If the student has misinterpreted the text he is responding to, explain why some readers might think that his understanding misses the point. That's why you have the computer for making critiques—so that you can elaborate enough to make your criticisms clear and useful, and the tone courteous.

20

Critiquing Compositions: Your Major Concerns

As you take up a piece of student writing for a critique, focus on these concerns in this order:

20-a Requirements

The first thing you want to determine about a student's draft of an essay (or part of an essay) is whether or not the student is fulfilling your requirements for the assignment. If you asked for a narrative essay presented in scenes with some dialogue and the student turned in a scene-less string of actions with no dialogue, you would indicate the problem at the outset of your response. Then you would delve into the text and find, by way of example, an appropriate place where the student might compose a scene or create some dialogue. Or you might create a "scene outline," a list of several scenes that would encompass the narrative he has written.

This may be enough of a response from you at this time. You are giving the student plenty of work to do for the next draft of the paper.

20-b Development

Your next concern after requirements is whether the student is adequately developing his topic. Suggest further development where you think it might be effective. For example, if the student is writing an argumentation essay and hasn't dealt with an important argument that is frequently made by those who disagree with the student's view, point this out. Indicate that if such arguments are not presented and answered, the reader may think that the writer is unaware of them. That can weaken the persuasive force of a whole essay.

Another general approach: Underline a phrase or sentence and suggest expanding it into a full paragraph, perhaps with a topic sentence.

Below is a numbered list of conventional "methods of development" (MDs) that you can hand out to your students (and publish online and keep on reserve in the library, for when they lose it). This allows you to simply write an MD-number (such as MD-3) in the margin indicating where you think one of these methods might usefully apply for further development. In your printed response sheet, you can expand on the MD suggestion, depending on how controlling you want to be. Early in the term you may want to make clear suggestions, such as those that appear in the numbered list below underneath each MD. Later in the term you may want to just put an MD-number in the margin and nothing more.

MD-1 Provide Descriptive Detail

You write that one kind of bad roommate keeps his side of the dorm room messy. Enhance your text and help your reader with a description of the mess—ash tray full of ashes and butts, clothes on the floor, unmade bed, books lying on the floor.

MD-2 List Examples

You write that some kinds of musical instruments are fairly easy to learn at the outset and some are particularly hard. The guitar is easy. Further enlighten your reader with a list of some of the other easy ones and some of the hard ones.

MD-3 Develop a Single Example

You say that there are several nice walks around town that one can take for exercise. Help the reader with a detailed description of a good trail.

MD-4 Provide Evidence

You have written that it's not true that American public schools are bad compared to those of other countries, so it is wrong to say that schools of education aren't producing good teachers. What the reader needs is evidence to support the premise about American schools not being bad in comparison with other schools. Also, evidence that teachers are being blamed for this "false problem." This will involve quoting sources.

MD-5 Explain How

You write that a student can achieve better grades by attending class and organizing his time. The reader may be wondering: How do you organize your time? How do you know what to put in a daily schedule?

MD-6 Explain Why

You say that girls get better grades than boys in high school. The reader may be wondering: Why is that so? Are they naturally smarter, or more focused on academics, or more obedient to the teacher's will? Such matters have been studied and the answers are out there.

MD-7 Show Similarities

You write that really good athletes in every sport have a will to win. What else do they have in common?

MD-8 Show Differences

You argue that a Laser is a good sailboat for young people because it goes fast. How else does it differ from other boats in ways that make it a good choice for the young?

[**Note:** You can show students how to make comparisons in blocks, all about A and then all about B (AAA BBB). Or point by point (AB AB AB).]

MD-9 Define Terms

You have written that your experience working with autistic children has resulted in your choosing special education as a major. What is an autistic child?

[You can introduce students to standard methods of definition. See 30-d (6).]

20-c *Complex Thinking*

Your next concern is depth of thinking. If a student isn't thinking deeply enough about his subject but is treating it in a simplistic manner, ask some challenging questions:

—What about the fact that Levin produces no real life examples of the kind of situation he says justifies torture? Is the situation that he imagines for the sake of argument likely to ever occur?

—What if the tortured agent gives a false location of the hidden nuclear device, in order to stop the torture? In other words, will torture even work?

When you play the devil's advocate, state that that is what you are doing—so the student doesn't think that this is your view and that he is offending you by disagreeing with you (otherwise he may change his view to conform with what he believes is yours). Say something like, "Let me take the other side of this argument and challenge some of the things you are saying." If you are typing your comments on your computer, as this book recommends, you can produce statements like that, something that is hard to do in the margins with a pen.

20-d Organization

Attend to issues of structure and the order of parts. The essay may be imbalanced, with a lot of discussion of one important issue and very little of another. Or you might see an advantage to a different order in the presentation of points. Explain your reasoning, e.g. "Your first point about motive seems to depend on your second point and is hard to understand without it. Consider presenting your second point first."

20-e Editing

Your final concern is with the quality of editing and proofreading. Some writers always edit as they write, but an editor (you) should turn to sentence errors only at the very end of the student's writing process. There is no point in forcing correction of a proofreading error or a grammatical mistake in a sentence if, after all revisions have taken place, that sentence won't even show up in the final version of the essay.

Your main approach to errors should be to flag them, not correct them. On rare occasions, you may want to write a short discussion in your word-processed comment sheet, when the fault is complex and the student would probably not be able to correct the problem on his own.

The writing guru Peter Elbow describes an approach in which the instructor puts a wavy line under awkward phrasing and a straight line under an error in grammar, punctuation, or usage (something that *must* be repaired).

You will be surprised at how good students are at fixing such problems with this kind of minimal help.

You can also put page and section numbers in the margin that refer the student to the place in the required handbook where an error is discussed. Or on the typed response sheet, write something like "7. Check your handbook for comma after an introductory element." Then use a pen to put a 7 in the margin. This teaches students to use reference books to answer questions about sentence-level issues, a habit that will serve them far beyond your composition course.

21

Critiquing Compositions: Efficiency

Make your responses as efficiently as possible so that repetitive drudge work is kept to a minimum and most of your energy can go into creative thinking.

21-a *Codes, Abbreviations, Page References*

When responding to student writing, you achieve two advantages from using codes like MD–6 or page numbers from a handbook. This approach speeds up your response time, always a good thing if there isn't any loss of quality. And it gives you flexibility in terms of how directive you want to be. You can drop down a code term and do nothing else, or you can include explanatory comments. You need to be directive enough for the student to understand your suggestion for improvement, but as minimally directive as possible so that the student can move toward independence.

Make sure that students know that if they don't understand a comment of yours they can ask you about it in your office or via e-mail.

21-b *Object Library*

The same problems and issues arise in student work again and again, and your response will be pretty much the same, with maybe a few word changes to fit the situation exactly. Gradually create a collection of well-constructed and nicely phrased comments that you can quickly cut and paste into your response sheet, making any necessary editing changes so that the pre-fabricated passage fits precisely with the student's text and what you want to say about it.

Technical writers call these passages "objects," which they keep in an "object library," and they use an "object-oriented" writing process as much as possible, meaning they construct texts as much as possible from passages that have already been worked out and refined. They do so because, as Murdick and Bloemker put it, "compared to texts created from scratch, object-oriented texts are quicker to write, they contain fewer factual and proofreading errors, and they exhibit more polished phrasing" (*The Portable Technical Writer*, Cengage). Take a tip from the pros. Over time, create and use a well-organized object library. It'll make your life easier and your responses better.

As you work through a stack of papers, create an open file on your computer and start saving "objects" that you find yourself using for this particular assignment, and then start using them in your responses to save time. Later you might add some to your permanent object library, which you can organize into sections for General Comments and for various particular assignments that you will repeat in future classes.

22

Writing Conferences

Some instructors prefer to talk to students orally about their drafts rather than critique them in written form. Or do both. Those instructors may call individual students up to the podium during class for a quick oral review, while the rest of the students are engaged in an in-class activity. Or the instructor might arrange for meetings in her office for more leisurely conferring.

Be warned that a *tête-à-tête* at the podium leaves you vulnerable to whatever viruses are circulating among the student population. Mononucleosis may be called the "kissing disease," but you don't have to get that close to pick it up. It's easy to imagine our colleagues in Asia conducting these conferences wearing face masks, as our dentists now do as they bend over the patient's face. Don't go that far, but consider the problem. It's real.

You should definitely plan to conduct writing conferences in your office while students are planning and composing the long research paper. In your office, you can sit safely across the desk from your visitor. The student brings to the meeting everything he has done so far and makes a presentation, to catch you up on his work. He talks about finding sources and what those sources are telling him. He reveals problems and asks questions.

Make sure that students know, ahead of time, what they are supposed to bring to conferences. This is especially applicable to the long research paper. Conferences help you keep track of how students are doing with this difficult assignment.

You can make a strong intervention when a student starts missing meetings and not turning in drafts of sections of the paper. Most likely the student is flummoxed by the task and needs extra help from you and the Writing Center. Don't wait—get on the errant student's case at the first sign that something is wrong.

23

Sentence Error: Politics and Pedagogy

23-a *The Problem*

The general public, school administrators, and faculty in other departments assume that English teachers are responsible for teaching students to write correctly, and they sometimes blame English departments when errors continue to arise in student work. In reality, English teachers can't do much in the way of teaching correctness. After all, if they could, they would, and errors would disappear from student writing.

Formal studies on the effects of direct instruction (lectures and drills) on sentence error in student papers began at the beginning of the 20th c. in the U.S. and continued throughout most of the century. The results were consistent: Teaching and drilling grammatical concepts and rules for correctness did not reduce error counts in student papers. For a review of this research, see Patrick Hartwell's "Grammar, Grammars, and the Teaching of Grammar" (*College English*, 47.2, 1985).

Students develop as stylists throughout college and beyond, gradually producing more complicated and sophisticated sentences. As they do so, error rates can actually rise. For example, if a writer begins to embed more text between the subject and verb, more subject-verb agreement errors are likely to occur—at least at first. What is clear is that people learn how to write correctly the sophisticated sentences they write as professional adults only after they have begun writing those kinds of sentences, not before. They routinely write those kinds of sentences and start obtaining control over them long after they have seen their last English teacher. They probably learn this information and acquire this ability through reading, which, after all, is the only significant contact people have with formal written English.

When you have time, you might read Richard Haswell's "Error and Change in College Student Writing" (*Written Communication* 1988, 479-99). If your library doesn't carry *Written Communication*, acquire the article through interlibrary loan. Haswell connects specific errors in student writing with specific style changes that signify syntactic growth. He concludes that heavy-handed attempts by English teachers to squash error may only retard the growth that must precede correctness.

Haswell's conclusion is backed by the many cases of students reverting to a primer style to defend themselves from the red pen. As a composition instructor, you want to encourage syntactic and lexical growth, not discourage it, even if that means more error in the short run.

Some instructors encourage students to write more complicated sentences through sentence combining exercises, in which the students are asked to combine two or three short sentences into a single long sentence. Courses which focus strongly on grammar and correctness drill often segue into sentence combining exercises, in which the grammatical terminology is put to use in giving instructions to students as to what structures to use in combining sentences. Early research on sentence combining showed that sentence combiners, when ask to write an essay in class, wrote more complicated sentences than did non-combiners doing the same assignment. However, later research revealed that students who had never done a sentence combining exercise in their life would write sentences just as complicated as those written by sentence combiners if they were prompted to do so. All the instructor had to do was tell the non-combiners that their grade will be higher if they wrote their essay in long complicated sentences. Of course, what writers need to learn is not how to write complicated structures, but how to write *effective* sentences that advance their rhetorical purpose. No one has come up with an exercise for that.

Generally speaking, forget exercises. At the very least, they have a tendency to consume too much valuable time. Focus your course on the writing of essays.

23-b Teach Processes for Reducing Error

Getting others to read one's work is an important editing process. Professional writers are always looking for people to read and comment on their texts. They hound their spouses and friends, and rely on their editors for feedback and proofreading. They know that the more critiquing they get, and the more they revise on the basis of those critiques, the better their final version will be. And the fewer errors will be left in print. So tell your students that the general rule is: Get as many critiques as you can.

Beyond that, you can teach proofreading and other techniques that students can use on their own:

(1) Suggest to your students that they read their texts aloud to themselves. This will often expose an awkward and possibly ungrammatical construction.

(2) Suggest reading a short text backwards, line by line from the bottom of the page upwards. This defeats the brain's natural tendency to read for meaning, a tendency that makes the reader "blind" to the letters and words and structures on the page. Reading backwards allows one to "see" the text.

(3) Suggest to students that they maintain an Error Notebook with the unique set of mistakes they individually make in their writings, such as misusing

comparatives and superlatives like *better* and *best* or putting a comma between the subject and predicate. Just maintaining the notebook and glancing through it before proofreading makes them alert to these problems. On occasion you might name an error that appears in a student's text and write E/N in the margin to suggest to the student that he include this error in his Error Notebook.

(4) After the warning about the uselessness of lectures and drills on correctness, this may sound like a contradiction, but there is some information about English that is quite learnable. For example, students can get a better handle on the Five Bugaboos, homophone mistakes that have been driving English teachers up the wall for two centuries:

> its / it's
> there / their / they're
> to / too
> of / have
> where / were

You can give quizzes on this kind of thing. You can ask groups to do a Bugaboo search on each other's text before turning their essays in to you for a critique.

Don't waste your time and the students' time by asking them to learn the difference between sixty homophone pairs. They will memorize the information for quizzes and then promptly forget it. Instead, have them look up a pair, like *affect* and *effect*, in their online dictionary as a homework assignment so they can see how to solve this problem on their own. Choose *a few* of the most commonly misused words for this purpose.

23. Sentence Error: Politics and Pedagogy

(5) Flag errors in students' essays as a starting point to their making corrections. To flag is to mark the location of an error without naming it or correcting it. Section 20-e above describes Peter Elbow's approach, which is worth repeating: The instructor puts a wavy line under awkward phrasing and a straight line under an error in grammar, punctuation, or usage (something that *must* be repaired). The student is then left to figure out how to revise. This minimalist approach is surprisingly effective. Students are almost always capable of figuring out what needs to be changed and how, even if they don't have the technical vocabulary for describing the error or stylistic infelicity.

(6) Put appropriate handbook page numbers in the margin where problems occur so that students practice learning from their handbook. During this activity, they will pick up some of the "vocabulary of error" in a way that is meaningful to them.

As a final note, there is nothing wrong with talking briefly about error and with showing students the kinds of errors that often arise in student writing. This kind of orientation to problems may be useful and might make their handbook slightly more comprehensible. Just don't assume that continued discussion and endless drilling will make those errors go away. That's not going to happen. That's not how the human brain learns this kind of information. If such methods did work, the problem would have been solved in 7th grade.

24

Portfolio Assessment

One traditional way of grading composition students is to assess their essays as they are submitted and then average the scores for the final grade. You might deduct a letter-grade to punish too many absences. Or you might find a way to figure in quiz and homework scores.

This text, however, assumes that you will not be doing that. Instead, it assumes that you will be using portfolio assessment. Under this system, students will not turn in individual papers for evaluation, but will turn in a set of written work, at least two and perhaps three times during the term, and you will give them one grade for each set or portfolio.

You don't have to operate this way, but there are good reasons for doing so. The main advantage of portfolio assessment is that it allows students to work on their final drafts right up until the day the portfolio is due. This supports a teaching/learning method centered on critique & revision. It also obviates the need to take attendance and enforce attendance policies, since quizzes and classwork are turned in so frequently that students always run a risk of losing portfolio points if they are not in class.

24-a Contents

A portfolio includes a set of critiqued drafts of essays, as well the final drafts of usually two to four essays. The portfolio also includes quizzes, homework, and classwork, all of which count toward the portfolio grade.

24. Portfolio Assessment

You may be wondering: In addition to grading essays, is it sensible, in a writing class, to give credit for activities such as quizzes, Writing Center visits, and homework? If you believe that those activities contribute to learning (and why else would you assign them?), then the answer is yes. You are giving credit for learning. Remember, you are there primarily to teach, not grade. Don't get your pants twisted up about grades. Anyone who is doing the work of your course is learning.

24-b Organization of Portfolios

During the term, you will return all quizzes, homework, and drafts of papers soon after their submission (usually the next class meeting), with your stamp or signature on them to validate that they were submitted on time. If you buy a date stamp for this purpose, that will help later when the portfolio material needs to be organized for submission and grading. (In addition, make sure that students date all their work throughout the term.) Buy an ink pad with an unusual color to thwart counterfeiting by some enterprising student.

Any work that you accept late will be marked "late" in whatever fashion you choose. You will eventually record points (give credit) for quizzes, any classwork that is collected, homework, and critiqued drafts. During the first portfolio period, you must repeatedly warn students to keep all their work for later submission in the portfolio, or they will not get credit for it and their portfolio grade will suffer.

Each piece of work should have a date and a title at the top, e.g. **Feb 12 – In class WTL on Procter essay**. You give them the titles for writing-to-learn activities done in class, such as the one in bold above. Having a date and title on every piece of work is absolutely crucial for organizing a portfolio for submission. You keep track of the portfolio content on your own makeshift Portfolio-Grading-Sheet, adding titles and dates of work as they come in. Your Portfolio-Grading-Sheet is a work-in-progress until the very end.

You will not grade drafts of papers as they are individually submitted for your critique during the term, but you will give points for submission of the draft for review (meaning that students lose points if they fail to turn in a draft). The drafts you return will contain your written comments; that is, your advice on how to revise. Some advice: Don't accept or critique drafts not turned in on time. Instead, require students who miss deadlines to take their papers to the Writing Center for critiques. Under this policy, they will earn fewer points toward their portfolio grade for this review. Impress upon students that in college classes, as well as in the workplace outside of school, deadlines are important.

The students will soon realize, also, that it hurts them to miss your critique, not only because of the loss of a couple of points, but because it will be you—not a Writing Center employee—who will ultimately be grading their essay. It never hurts to point this out. Once your students realize that, they will work hard to meet the deadlines for submitting their drafts to you.

Students must keep all returned work in a manila folder with their name, group number, phone number, and e-mail address on the cover. In the center, in large writing, they should put: "If found, please contact me." This is their portfolio. Make sure everyone is using the same simple manila folder—it makes for easier carrying for you. Show them one. (You might even give them away free.) You will put the portfolio grade on the inside back cover. At the end of the term there will be grades there for each portfolio, and students can figure out what final grade they will be getting in the course.

To repeat, for each portfolio, you are giving point credits for:

—quizzes
—homework
—classwork that has been turned in

24. Portfolio Assessment

—each required draft of a paper that has been critiqued

—each final draft of a paper, based on your evaluation of its quality.

24-c Grading Portfolios

As indicated, the final draft of each paper will be graded on quality (see Chapter 26, Grading Papers). Just to keep the math easy for you to do and easy for the students to understand, you can make the point values for quizzes, homework, classwork, and drafts add up to 50 percent of the portfolio grade, or 50 points. Then average the paper grades and count that average grade 50 percent. So if a student has an 80 average on final copies, the student gets 40 points. For the student's portfolio grade, you would add the number 40 to the points accumulated from the other work. Of course, if you want to put a different value on final drafts—say, 75 percent—you will have to multiply the paper-grade average by .75 and make the value of the remaining work add up to 25 points. You can give more value to some papers than others using similar math.

To allow for a few absences from class, you can drop one or two of the lowest quiz grades and allow for one or two missed in-class WTLs. Each quiz might be worth 2 or 3 points, depending on how many questions there are. It's best if all quizzes are worth the same number of points. Say 3. If you ask 6 questions, you can count each question $1/2$ a point. If you ask 4 questions, you can instruct students to pick 3 to answer and give 1 point credit for each correct answer.

Here's another example of flexible math. Let's say that you want to give 10 pts for getting required critiques from you and the writing center, and the students are supposed to have two critiques of each of three papers, or six critiques total. If you give 1 pt for each critique, the most a student could earn would be 6 pts, not 10. If you give 2 pts for your critique and 1 pt for the writing center critique, that would add up to only 9 pts. If you give 2 pts for each critique, that will add up to 12 pts if the student did all the work. How are you going to get the magic number 10? Here's the solution. For that section of the portfolio evaluation, give 2 pts per critique but declare that the maximum points earnable for this section is 10. So a student only has to submit 5 of the 6 critiques to earn full credit for this section. This may be a little screwy, but it is screwy in a way that makes it easier for students to get good grades. Never bend the laws of math in ways that make it more difficult for students to score well.

Don't like students getting full credit if they missed a critique? Here's another solution. Make this section worth 12 pts instead of 10 and take away 2 pts from some other section.

And remember through all this, grades are important only to students. They are not important to you, or to the known Universe.

24-d *Sequencing the Evaluation of Work*

In a basic writing ("remedial") course, normally students will be writing more drafts of fewer papers, since it will take them longer to produce something that looks like a college essay. Their first portfolio might consist of all the work that goes into the production of a single essay. In a regular composition course, a single portfolio might contain anywhere from two to four essays in final form, along with drafts and other work done for credit.

The credits for homework, classwork, and drafts can lift the grade of a weak writer, but that's OK. Almost all weak writers will improve as the course proceeds. The third portfolio can be set up to give more credit for quality of final copies and less for the other work. Let's say, 25 pts for each of three papers (75 pts total) and 25 pt for the rest. The writers who were originally weak but hard working should be able to score decently on that kind of portfolio scale by the end of the term.

24. Portfolio Assessment

24-e Lost Portfolios

What happens if a student loses his portfolio and all the work in it? This is when you earn your high teacher pay. First, a lot of the student's work, especially the essays, should exist on his computer in draft form. Allow him to print those drafts and revise essays and put them in a folder to create a slimmed down portfolio.

You should have a pretty good idea if the student has been turning in work all along and even a vague idea of how good his essays were. That should influence your degree of generosity. If you know that the student has been screwing off and not turning in a lot of the work, you can put a limit of a C or D grade for this portfolio. If you know the student has been doing the work faithfully and isn't a bad writer, you can accept the reduced portfolio and grade it on the merits of the essays alone, forgetting all the rest. Another alternative is to tell the student that you will determine his final grade entirely on the average score of the other two portfolios submitted during the term and give him no grade on the lost portfolio.

25

A Sample Portfolio Grading Sheet

Make up an evaluation sheet for the portfolio that is about to be submitted and give it out to students before the portfolio is due, so that they can organize the material in their portfolios. You want them to physically stack up their paperwork consistently with the list of items on the evaluation sheet. You don't want to have to shuffle through a big stack of papers looking to see if a student took a particular quiz or turned in a particular in-class paragraph.

On the sheet, number each item. For example: **#11 Levin (WC)**, which means that this item is the draft of the student's response to the Levin essay which was critiqued by a Writing Center (WC) tutor. (The tutor's signature should appear on the draft.) Ask students to put the same numbers on their pieces of work and put them in order in the folder. If a piece is missing, ask the student to indicate that fact on the grade sheet you have given them to organize their work. They would do this by putting an X in the line to the left where the grade points would go. Otherwise, you will waste time looking for the item. Other than that, students should not mark any other lines for recording points; you will be the one to put numbers (credit points) in those lines.

When the students turn in their portfolios, their grade sheet should be on top.

A draft which was critiqued by the student's group during class should have one or more Critique Sheets stapled to it (consider bringing staplers to class). A draft that you critiqued should have your markings and a comment sheet stapled to it. Other work can be identified by the date the student has put on it at the time of doing it.

Figure 2 provides a model grading sheet for a portfolio.

Figure 2: A Sample Portfolio Grading Sheet

Comp I   First Portfolio Grade: ___

Essay Grades (60 pts/20 pts each) Total Earned: ____

____ #1 Narrative Essay
____ #2 Informative Essay
____ #3 Response to Levin

Critiqued Drafts (18 pts/2 pts each) Total Earned: _____

____ #4 Narrative (Group Critique /GC)
____ #5 Narrative (Writing Center Critique/ WC)
____ #6 Narrative (Instructor's critique/IC)
____ #7 Informative (GC)
____ #8 Informative (WC)
____ #9 Informative (IC)
____ #10 Levin (GC)
____ #11 Levin (WC)
____ #12 Levin (IC)

Coursework (22 pts) Total Earned: ____

Homework (1 pt each/5 pts max)

___ #13 Sept 2   ___ #14 Sept 12   ___ #15 Sept 25
___ #16 Sept 29 ___ #17 Oct 1   ___ #18 Oct 3

In-class work (1 pt each/5 pts max)

____ #19 Sept 4   ____ #20 Sept 11   ____ #21 Sept 22
____ #22 Sept 30 ____ #23 Oct 1   ____ #24 Oct 3

Quizzes (3 pts each/12 pts max)

____ #25 Sept 3   ____ #26 Sept 11 ____ #27 Sept 22
____ #28 Sept 30 ____ #29 Oct 1

26

Grading Individual Papers

For most composition teachers, grading papers is the most repugnant part of their job. The methods described below may make the process somewhat easier for you and fairer to your students.

26-a Holistic Grading

You grade a paper holistically when you read it straight through and promptly put a grade on it. This should be the normal way to grade student compositions, except for the long research paper. Holistic grading is fast, and it is realistic in that you read to get an immediate general impression, which is what you do when you read a short article in a magazine. You are judging students on the same basis you would a professional writer—on what they have produced as a whole.

In your first paper-grading session, read three or four papers without grading them and then put them on the bottom of the pile to be read and graded last. This will give you a sense of what's coming your way, of what your students are capable of. If it's shocking, go get a cup of coffee and a chocolate donut before continuing.

No pen in your hand. Read each paper as you would that article in a magazine. Then put your grade on it or record the appropriate number of points in the portfolio grading sheet. Make no comments on A and B papers. You might write a *very short* note on papers receiving C or below indicating anything the student did well and what the student needs to work on in the future. If a student wants to know more, and occasionally one will, he can meet with you in your office during your office hours. Beyond that, you have to assume that learning is over once a paper has been graded. Don't waste a lot of time marking up a paper that won't be revised.

26-b Analytical Grading

For analytical grading, you put together a list of characteristics to be evaluated and give separate grades on each of those characteristics. You may give them different weights or values. You would then turn that list of grades into a single grade for the paper.

This is how papers are often graded when social scientists do educational research; however, they have more time than the typical harried composition instructor. Nevertheless, it is probably how you should grade the long research paper that students typically write during the second half of the second regular course in a composition program. Such essays typically run about ten or more pages and have ten or more bibliography entries. Besides grading the content, you would want to give separate grades on the use of sources, the use of quotations, and bibliographic form, among other features. Figure 5 in section 35-j provides an example of an analytical grading sheet for such a paper.

26-c Primary Trait Grading

Normally, the analytical approach is too time consuming to be practical for routine paper evaluation. However, a method called Primary Trait grading can be used to create a minimal analytical grading sheet that can be usable for routine short essays. In Primary Trait grading, you determine

26. Grading Individual Papers

the most important distinctive trait of a particular type of essay. For a narrative essay, you might decide that the most important feature to evaluate is the ability to tell a story in scenes or the ability to make meaning out of an experience. Or both. You might then give the essay a primary trait grade on each of those traits, and then combine those evaluations into one grade for the paper. For example:

___ (50 pts) Use of scenes to tell the story

___ (50 pts) Drawing meaning from the experience

Don't keep these criteria a secret. Make sure students see your grading sheet before the deadline for the first draft, so that right from the start they can set and pursue goals for this assignment.

27

Day One in Class

Give students a couple of extra minutes to get to class. Some of them will be searching for the classroom. Announce the name of the course and write it on the blackboard so that anyone who is in the wrong room can leave immediately in search of the right room.

OK, you're ready to start the term.

27-a Take Attendance

Ask students with difficult names to help you pronounce them correctly. Take notes on pronunciation. Some students in the room may not be on your list; make sure it is because they registered late. If they registered on time, tell them to visit the registrar's office after class to straighten things out.

27-b Distribute The Syllabus and Introduce the Course

Hand out copies of your syllabus. Give a short lecture on the writing program at your school and on the nature of this course, even if your syllabus covers that information. Many students do not read syllabi. Your name and contact information should be in the top line of the first page of the syllabus—they will read that much. Discuss required textbooks. Tell students to bring to class everyday a notebook to be used in this course, or at least a section in a notebook

27. Day One in Class

reserved for this course. Tell them they will need their notebooks at the next class meeting.

Discuss your classroom policies. Read them from the syllabus. State that there will be a quiz on them at the beginning of the next class meeting.

27-c Introduce the Writing Center

Explain what a writing center is and how you intend to have them use it. Include its location and hours, even if that information is in your syllabus.

27-d Discuss Portfolio Assessment

Besides giving oral instructions, you should also include a description of this assessment method in your syllabus, emphasizing the need for students to *save everything*. State that one of the quiz questions at the next class meeting will be on what goes into a portfolio.

27-e Explain Your Policy on Quizzes, In-class Work, and Homework

Make sure the students understand that there will be a quiz on every, or almost every, reading assignment, starting with the next class. Put a positive light on it. Explain that quizzes will be no problem for anyone who has read the assignment and that quizzes allow students to easily build up points toward their portfolio grades. However, note that quizzes will be given in the first few minutes of the class, and there is no make-up, even for "legitimate" absences. So it is unwise to be late for class. Indicate that you will drop one or two of the lowest quiz scores when compiling grades, to allow for absences.

Also, explain that you give points for in-class work that you collect and homework turned in on time.

27-f Introduce the First Writing Assignment

Explain the first writing task and get them started through an assignment. If the students have a reader and they are going to write an essay in response to reading, assign pages of reading. If the essay is particularly long, you might assign the first half of it. Warn the students that at least one of the questions for the quiz next time will come from the reading.

Note: If this is a night class (3 hours) or a long day class (1 ½ hours), you will need to get them started on their first writing task in class, perhaps beginning with a WTL activity followed by class discussion and then some writing. If that is the case, then do the next activity, 27-g, *before* this one, 27-f. Have them do the writing sample described below, which you will keep, and then perhaps form temporary groups and begin working on the first essay.

For a long class, you might give a lecture on the essay type, discussing its main features, and then read aloud a short sample essay. Suppose, for example, the students will be writing a personal narrative essay as their first assignment. You might ask them to listen to this essay that you are going to read and note how it is composed of a series of scenes and how important dialogue is to the development of the story and the characters.

27-g Administer Diagnostic Tests/Surveys

Note: Either 27-g or 27-h can be done on Day Two, if there isn't time in the first class period.

Diagnostic tools are administered at the beginning of the term and again at the end. For a writing class, they provide you with information about your students' growth (or lack thereof) in work habits and attitudes.

First ask your students to write a paragraph on their personal writing process: How do you go about writing a paper or an important message? What do you do first? When and where do you write? Do you compose the first draft by hand or on a computer? How long do you spend on the project? What do you do with the draft when it is finished? Do you check spelling? Edit it in some other way? **Note:** You can formalize this by creating a sheet which asks specific questions (fill in the blank) or which offers multiple choice or T/F answers. E.g., "T/F I spend more time re-writing than writing."

Don't use a standardized instrument; make up your own. Get into teacher-research!

You should also administer an attitude survey to find out how your students' attitudes change over the term. Will they become more positive and sophisticated? If so, you have succeeded in an important way. You might look at the Daly-Miller attitude survey, which is available on the Web, and then make up your own simpler survey. For your first term, you might use the one in Figure 3.

Here's one way to handle it. Ask students to fill in the survey, noting that there are no right or wrong answers, just honest and dishonest ones. Urge them to be honest. After they have taken the survey, ask them to then add up the numbers in the column and put the sum in the Total blank. They should also record that number in their writing notebooks.

You later total all the numbers in the Total blanks to get a class total, and divide that by the number of surveys to get a class average. At the end of the term, administer the same survey and get the average score for comparison. You hope the score average goes up noticeably, since that is partly a measure of your success. A positive attitude toward an activity leads to more learning; a negative attitude can decrease learning.

Figure 3: A Writing Attitude Survey

How much do you agree or disagree with these statements about your attitude towards writing? Write an appropriate number in each blank.

4 – Strongly agree   3 – Agree   2 – Disagree   1 – Strongly disagree

____ I think writing is an important skill for almost all professions

____ I enjoy having other people read the things I write

____ I am confident about my ability to express my thoughts clearly in writing

____ I like the idea of taking a writing course because writing is enjoyable for me

____ I usually have no trouble getting started when I have to write something

____ I am confident my sentences are pretty much free of errors in grammar, punctuation, and capitalization

____ Total

Note: Professional surveys would mix up positively expressed statements (I look forward to writing a paper) with negatively expressed statements (I dread writing a paper). This adds little to the authenticity of results and it makes scoring more difficult. It isn't worth the trouble for your purposes.

27-h Get a Writing Sample

Assuming you are teaching a 1-hour class, ask students to write for the remainder of the class describing their home

27. Day One in Class

town (or invent another subject). If this is a long class, give them 15-20 minutes for this task. Tell them to take a couple of minutes to plan what they are going to say, and then begin writing.

Do not ever return these samples. Keep them on file in case you have a plagiarism problem with a student that turns into a dispute that ends up in the dean's office. Plagiarism happens, and students can be gutsy (or extremely naïve) about denying it. When Steve Student denies your plagiarism charge and insists that he wrote all of his own paper, it helps to be able to show your dean a sample of his infantile prose done in class, which can be compared to the piece of brilliant professional-level writing that he is now calling his own.

28

Evening One at Home

28–a Use the Writing Samples to Create Groups

Divide the sample papers into three groups: 1) far better than average, 2) far worse than average, and 3) everyone else. Group #3 should include most of the students, with only a few falling into the other categories. You want to identify the truly weak students and the strong ones who can help them when you create groups.

Create classroom workgroups of four to five students each. Mix men and women, strong and weak. Try not to put more than one weak student in a group. If there are two weak writers in a group, at least one of the other two students should be strong.

28-b Create a Seating Chart

Your seating chart will consist of a simple pattern of numbers (e.g. 1-5), each number representing a group of four to five students. You will put the numbers on the blackboard at the beginning of the next class. Put Group 1 in the front near the door and your desk. Put Group 2 in the other position in the front. Put Group 3 in the middle of the room. Put Groups 4 and 5 in the back. The chart you put on the blackboard will look like this (assuming five groups):

28. Evening One at Home

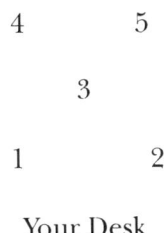

Your Desk

Your personal copy of the chart will have the names of the students in each group.

28-c *Prepare the Quiz*

Make the questions easy for any student who has read the material the quiz is based on. You can make two versions, A and B, if you worry about cheating. Same questions but different order of multiple choice answers—something like that. You can save paper by printing two on a page and cutting the pages in half, but don't make them smaller than half a page or they tend to get lost. Remember, these are going in their portfolio after you have graded and returned them, and they must not lose them.

Note: If you want to give two points for this quiz, you can ask three questions and ask them to answer only two. Or four questions and give a value of ½ pt for each.

28-d *Obtain a Packet of 3X5 Cards*

These will serve as information cards about your students.

28-e Prepare Activities Related to the First Writing Assignment

This may consist of discussion of an essay (after students have written in class on some question you raise about the essay). Or if your students will be writing from personal experience and perhaps some research, you can work with them on choosing a topic.

28-f Arrange a Library Tour

At some point early on, you are going to want to take your students on a tour of the library, or arrange a tour with library personnel. So walk over or call over and talk to the librarian who does the tours.

It is important to do this early on, so that your students can begin enhancing their writing with research right from the start. You don't want them to rely solely on the Internet. Too many books and journal articles and even newspaper articles are not online. The Internet is still too weak a database for extensive serious research. This will certainly change someday, but we're not there yet.

29

Day Two in Class

29-a Put Students into Groups

Take roll, this time assigning each student a Group number. You should take roll for the first week or so until you have learned the students' names. Put the seating chart (the pattern of group numbers) on the blackboard or whiteboard. Ask students to get up and re-seat themselves according to group location.

29-b Give the Quiz

Tell students to write their group number below their name on their quiz (and every other piece of work they hand in during the term). Also, ask them to put the date on it. This is a good time to tell them, or remind them, to date everything they turn in to you; indeed, everything they turn in to other professors throughout college and everything they write in the workplace after college.

When you return the quizzes at the beginning of the next class meeting, you will do so in batches to each group. Then the groups will distribute them. It saves time.

You do not need to record quiz grades because they will be turned in with the portfolio. Remind the students of that—that the grades are not yet recorded, but will be when the portfolio is submitted for a grade.

29-c Get Student Information

Tell students in each group to introduce themselves, so that each student has the following information on every other student (write this on the board): Full name, hometown, major, phone, e-mail, and class/work schedule. The class schedule and work schedule (for those who have jobs) will reveal times when each student is free for meetings or group work outside of class.

You can do it this way: Hand out 3X5 cards and ask students to write their information on a card, each fact on a separate line, and then pass the cards around the group so that each student can copy all the information on group members into his class notebook. Then collect the cards so that *you* have this information.

Or, print out a sufficient number of sheets of paper with the categories of information on it:

Name:

Hometown:

Major:

[etc.]

For the class/work schedule, students can put C's and W's in a grid to indicate times they are in <u>c</u>lass or <u>w</u>orking:

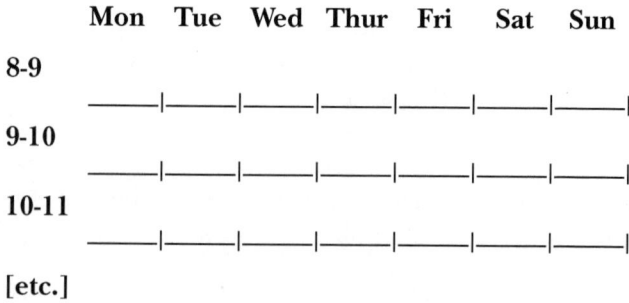

29. Day Two in Class

Or students can create a simpler chart which is less visually clear but does the trick:

Mon: C 9-11, 1-2 **W** 3-5

Tue: C 10-11:30, 1:00-2:30

[etc.]

Point out that if a student misses a class, that student can contact a group member to find out if there will be a quiz at the next class meeting or if any reading or written work will be due. There's a tradition in high school that if a student is absent, he is not responsible for turning in work that is due on the day he returns. Make it clear that in college students are responsible for turning in work on time regardless of absences.

29-d Assign Group leaders

If you are going to have students do any classwork today, ask each group to select a leader for the day. This person keeps the rest of the group on task when doing in-class work and reports to the whole class on what the group has come up with for ideas or conclusions. Today, the group leader will be the person with the most comfortable-looking shoes.

OK, now do what you prepared for this second day.

Part II

Teaching Six Types of Essay

The Five Paragraph Theme

The Personal Narrative

The Informative or Instructional Article

The Argument on a Controversial Issue

The Literary Criticism Essay

The Long Research Paper

30

The Five Paragraph Theme

30-a What It Is

The term "five paragraph theme" is the traditional name for a short essay focused on one main thought or theme, which is stated in a "thesis sentence." The thesis is developed through a three-part structure: (1) an introductory paragraph, (2) three to five paragraphs in the body of the theme, and (3) a concluding paragraph.

The introductory paragraph typically leads up to the thesis statement, though that key sentence might show up anywhere in the paragraph, including the first sentence. Each paragraph in the body usually begins with a "topic sentence," which functions as the thesis for that paragraph. Each topic sentence directly supports the main thesis. The rest of the sentences in a paragraph in the body may serve as sub-topic sentences which directly support the topic sentence idea. A sub-topic sentence may be followed by sentences that directly develop *it* rather than the topic sentence.

This kind of very tight relevance requirement for all sentences produces what is called "organic unity." Such paragraphs are called "organic paragraphs."

The example in Figure 4 comes from *A Student Guide to College Composition*, 2nd ed. (Jain Publishing). The thesis sentence at the end of the first paragraph and the topic sentences at the beginning of the paragraphs in the body are in boldface.

Figure 4: Sample Five Paragraph Theme

The Two Backhands in Tennis

By Steve Student

Since the 1970s, the two-handed backhand has become very popular in tennis. In recent years, you may have seen Rafael Nadal pounding two-handers for winners on his way to becoming Wimbledon champ. On the other hand, you may have also seen Roger Federer blasting traditional one-handed backhands on his way to winning major championships. Both strokes are widely used, and some players use both. This doesn't mean that they are essentially the same shot. **In fact, they are quite different.**

The one-handed backhand is a true backhand shot, but the two-hander is not. A player like Federer, in executing the one-handed shot, will turn his back to the approaching ball and swing backwards toward the net with his right arm. For Nadal, however, the backhand is actually a left-handed forehand, dominated by the left arm and wrist. Because Nadal, like most right-handed players, has never learned to hit a one-armed left-handed forehand shot, he uses his right arm and hand to steady the racket. If Nadal's right hand weren't stabilizing the forward motion of the racket, the racket head would wobble, making the shot impossible.

The shots are different also in terms of how the players position themselves for executing the stroke. One-handed Federer hits the ball further away from his body than two-handed Nadal does. Keeping both hands on the racket reduces the distance Nadal can stretch the racket away from his body. Federer gets his back to the ball at the outset of the motion and Nadal stands sideways, or even faces slightly open toward the oncoming ball.

Finally, the follow through for the top spin shot is different for each player. Federer stays down through the shot, keeping his knees bent. Nadal rises up. Federer finishes with the racket head high, pointing to the sky. Nadal follows through by twisting his body and swinging the racket fully over his shoulder.

Although these shots are both called "backhands," they are significantly different. Yet both are used by professionals today to effectively handle baseline shots.

30-b Relevance to Real Writing

This pattern of organization was invented by a Scottish logician in the 19th c. as an idealized scheme for writing. It was never popular in Scotland, but it became a big hit in America and even today remains one of the most common writing assignments in college composition classes. It may be part of your department's syllabus.

Five paragraph themes are virtually non-existent outside of English classrooms. This is not how professional writers produce essays and articles. Organic paragraphs do show up, most often in technical writing, but they are mainly the result of a writer's tendency to make a point and then back it up, explain it, or in some other way discuss it before starting a new paragraph—rather than a deliberate attempt to create organic paragraphs. It has been noted and confirmed through experiments that, in a fluent piece of prose, one can start a new paragraph after almost any sentence, and that break will seem natural. On reading over their text, professional writers will break up a long passage into two or more paragraphs to provide visual and mental relief. An accident of such paragraphing can leave behind an organic paragraph, and that's usually how they come into being.

30-c Usefulness

One rationale for teaching the five paragraph theme is that it forces students to stick around and develop their points instead of rushing from one point to the next. And you can usefully use this type of writing for just that purpose. In fact, even if your students are writing fuller essays and not five paragraph themes, you can suggest to a student whose paper lacks detailed development of points to turn a particular sentence that you have underlined into a topic sentence and create a whole paragraph around it, as a way of deepening development.

30-d Topics for Writing

Here are some options:

1) Students can write in response to your penetrating question about an essay they have read, such as Martin Luther King's "I Have a Dream" speech. A possible question: "What are the most important (or surprising or controversial) statements that Dr. King made in this speech? Why?"

2) Students can write an essay inspired by, or in imitation of, a reading. For example, "Write your own 'I Have a Dream' speech about some aspect of American life."

3) Students can invent their own subjects based on their personal experiences and expertise. (See 32-a for more on such topics.)

4) You can list broad topics for students to choose from as a starting point, such as Winning/Losing in Afghanistan, Lady Gaga, Choosing a College Major, Apple vs Microsoft, best woman athlete, vegetarianism, my worst/best teacher. Provide fifty of these so you don't have to deal with students who can't think of anything to write about. Then show them how to narrow down and put their own twist on the subject, producing a topic sentence: *The enemy will win in Afghanistan because we can't stay forever / Lady Gaga is a good role model for today's teenagers.*

5) The "methods of development" (MDs) listed in 20-b can also provide the starting point for assignments. E.g., "Compare or contrast your high school writing experiences with your college writing experiences."

For your own background, you might consult William Murdick's textbook *Writing and Reasoning* (Jain Publishing), which provides in-depth discussion of the kinds of reasoning inherent in ten standard MDs. Other composition textbooks provide relevant information as well.

6) Students can write an extended definition of an abstract word (e.g., *patriotism; socialism; a good boss*) or a technical term, such as *cloud computing*. This is a favorite assignment for paragraph-length pieces of writing, and it's a good exercise, because defining is an activity that arises in the course of many types of writing. Here is a list of standard methods of definition from Murdick's *A Student Guide to College Composition*, which students can draw upon in writing an extended definition:

> **Classification and differentiation:** A catamaran is a boat with two hulls.
>
> **Etymology** (word history): The word *computer* comes from the Latin word *computare* meaning "to count."
>
> **Negative definition:** Phonics is not a method of reading, but of word identification.
>
> **Contrast:** Terriers are more hyperactive than most other breeds.
>
> **Comparison** (similarities): Both a cable TV system and a satellite system will provide many channels.
>
> **Figurative comparison:** Health food is like medicine, only less expensive and without side effects.
>
> **Example:** Reference books for writers include dictionaries, spelling dictionaries, thesauruses, and word finders.

> **Purpose:** A trip report allows you to share with your supervisors and co-workers what you learned or accomplished on your trip.
>
> **Physical description:** Terriers tend to have short curly hair.
>
> **Operational description** (how it works): A vector graphic produces an image through the application of a mathematical formula defining the boundaries of the shape.
>
> **Components:** A progress report tells the reader how far along you are in the project, what problems you've been having, and what you plan to do next.

30-e Teaching the Structure of the Short Theme

Courses that require five paragraph themes usually focus heavily on grammar study and sentence error drills. Sometimes they also add sentence combining to the mix. These activities take up much of the course, because there isn't a lot of rhetoric to teach in regard to the short theme, but below are some ideas.

1) To start with, teach the topic-sentence controlled one-paragraph essay. Have students start with an enumerative topic sentence and then support it with three to five subtopic sentences, each one independently expanding on the topic sentence. An enumerative topic sentence indicates how many points are going to be made in the paragraph. This is the kind of essay you will be looking for:

> We should get our troops out of Afghanistan for three reasons. First, we have accomplished our missions there as well as we are going to. Second, it is costing us a lot of money

in these hard economic times. Finally, it is still a dangerous place for American soldiers and we don't want any more being killed for no good reason.

In this kind of mini-essay, or organic paragraph, you can often change the order of the subtopic sentences without harm, because they are independent. For example, here is the above paragraph with the second and third points switched:

> We should get out of Afghanistan for three reasons. First, we have accomplished our missions there as well as we are going to. Second, it is still a dangerous place for American soldiers and we don't want any more being killed for no good reason. Finally, it is costing us a lot of money in these hard economic times.

2) Next, show students how a subtopic sentence can be further developed with sentences loyal to it rather than to the topic sentence. Here's an expansion of the above paragraph with the subtopic development in bold:

> We should get out of Afghanistan for three reasons. First, we have accomplished our missions there as well as we are going to. **The Taliban have been beaten down, if not altogether defeated, and that's the best we'll ever do.** Second, it is still a dangerous place for American soldiers and we don't want any more being killed for no good reason. **The American death toll for this year is over 2,000.** Finally, it is costing us a lot of money in these hard economic times. **This past year we spent over $220 billion.**

3) Teach students that all essays can be enhanced by research, even a one paragraph theme. The statistics that appear in bold above came from charts easily found on the Web.

4) Moving to the multi-paragraph structured theme (aka the five paragraph theme), provide examples of introductory paragraphs whose thesis sentence is situated at the beginning, the middle, and the end. Ask students to re-write paragraphs you provide, changing the position of the thesis.

5) Show that topic sentences can have a dual function: to transition away from the previous topic and to introduce the next topic:

> **Although Iraq is a burgeoning democracy, it is still a dangerous place for Western advisors.**

The writer is signaling to the reader that the text is finished with the discussion of Iraqi democracy and is now going to take up the issue of danger for Westerners.

6) The body of the short theme consists of topic-sentence controlled paragraphs that directly develop the thesis. If the paper began with an enumerated thesis sentence, it is important that the paragraphs take up the listed topics in the order in which they were enumerated.

7) If the thesis sentence doesn't indicate exactly how it will be developed, the student can use the MDs in 20-b for ideas. Various conventions of ordering can also be considered:

- —chronological (ordered by time: first this happens, then this . . . etc.)
- —easiest to understand to most difficult to understand
- —familiar to unfamiliar
- —shortest (quickly covered) to longest (requires more development)
- —most interesting or important to least interesting or important (because readers will stop reading the text if they get bored early)

30. The Five Paragraph Theme

> —least important to most important (to end strongly)
>
> —visual (close up to far away; far away to close up; around the outside; inside to out; outside to in; left to right or right to left; high to low or low to high).

8) The concluding paragraph of a short theme usually reviews the main idea and important support that the writer has provided. In other words, it summarizes. But you can suggest other slants and possibilities. Here are some from Murdick's *A Student Guide to College Composition, 2nd Ed.*:

> —Restate and elaborate on the importance of the subject.
>
> —Restate the main point, now not as something you will prove, but as the logical conclusion from what you've said about the topic (e.g., Judging by the experience of Pumpkinville College, it seems clear that the best way to reduce the occurrence of date rape is by educating both men and women on what constitutes date rape and the circumstances that lead to it).
>
> —Mention other texts (books or magazines or Web resources) the reader might consult for more information on the topic.
>
> —Indicate what remains unknown about the subject and where further research needs to be done.
>
> —Make a prediction about the future based on what you have written (e.g., Within our lifetime, we will probably see the end of the internal combustion engine in automobiles).
>
> —Give a warning (e.g., Never be casual about taking measurements during a construction job. As we have seen, the consequences of even the slightest error can be disastrous).

—Make a hopeful statement (e.g., The major problems of dentistry have been solved. We know what people need to do to care for their teeth. As dentists get better at communicating that information to their patients, we can expect more and more people to retain all of their teeth for all of their life).

—Call for action (e.g., Parents of school children in every community should insist, loudly, that their schools do not give up their full, rich curriculum for the limited focus of test-preparation drills).

31

The Personal Narrative Essay

The most important task in teaching the personal narrative is to move students along from merely recounting a chain of events to creating a memoir that develops through scenes towards a climax and denouement. Events, in other words, must develop through description, dialogue, and action to somewhere meaningful. Judith Barrington, in her book *Writing the Memoir: From Truth to Art*, puts it this way:

> Rather than simply telling a story from her life, the memoirist both tells the story and muses upon it, trying to unravel what it means in the light of her current knowledge.

Students can make themselves the main focus of their narrative, or someone else, such as a favorite aunt. In the latter case, the student would appear as a minor character, though one who is probably influenced by the main character being described. It remains a "personal" narrative because the student writer is struggling to capture and understand someone important to him personally.

31-a Sample Writing Topics

Supply your students with a list of possible topics for a narrative essay, the more the better. The Web can help you. Search "topics for personal narrative essays." In the meantime, here are a few ideas to get you started:

—Write on an enlightening experience you have had since coming to this campus. What did you learn?

—Relate the story of a trip you once took that showed you something about life in general or about people or about a person (maybe yourself).

—Write about a relative of yours who has taught you something about how to live.

—Describe a bad experience in your life. What did you learn? What did you gain or lose? How did it change you?

—Describe an event that you read about—a big event in the world or a small story—that changed the way you look at certain things and changed your behavior.

—Describe the oddest person you have encountered. What did this person teach you about human nature or about yourself?

—Describe one of your teachers who had a strong effect on your life.

31-b Narrative Structure

A personal narrative essay, though non-fiction, should deploy the same elements that a novel does: exposition, description, dialogue, action. Point out these elements in whatever personal narrative essays your students read as models. Virtually every scene in a well-written narrative essay contributes to characterization of the main figures in the story. Show how this occurs in the model essays. After demonstrating, ask students to analyze model essays in that fashion.

Narrative essays contain the following structures, and you can request that students follow this simple pattern for their first draft:

31. The Personal Narrative Essay

—Background
—Episode
—Commentary

Students can write, and submit for your review, each of those elements separately.

31-c Background

Ask the students to include in the background, along with actions, the following information: Time, place, and characters. Background can be usefully seen as either broad and distant or recent and focused. Distant is optional; recent and focused may be necessary.

Distant background may discuss a situation or events that took place before the protagonist (possibly the student writer) appears as a character in the narrative. It is history. Recent background covers the situation leading up to the episode at the heart of the essay. It may be the precipitator of events. Or it may provide information necessary for understanding the main events of the narrative.

31-d Episode

Ask students to include in the episode physical description of people and locations, physical action, and verbal action or dialogue. They have all seen TV narrative programs, like a situation comedy. Note that these programs proceed by scenes. The TV screen goes black for a fraction of a second and suddenly we are in a different location with perhaps new characters conversing with the protagonist. An episode may be put together as a series of such scenes. Or it can be one long scene. Make sure that the students know their options. And make sure that they understand that the episode should be an event meaningful to the narrator (the student writer), an event that finishes something, or starts something, or reveals something in the narrator's life.

31-e Commentary

The narrator's understanding of the meaningfulness of the event is conveyed through commentary, which in our simple structure would come last. In one common type of commentary, the writer reveals a sudden understanding of something right after the final climax. That unraveling of the "meaning of it all" is called the denouement. A professional essayist might leak some commentary during the episode or even before it begins. However, for a first attempt at this genre by first-year college students, a simple structure in which the elements remain separate works well, at least for the first draft. If you want to complicate the structure a bit, have students write a short epilogue: How has the learning affected you many years later?

32

The Informative Essay

The informative essay educates the reader on some subject, or it instructs the reader on how to do something. Students pass on expertise gained from experience and personal education, including research. This assignment is a particularly good context within which to teach audience awareness and analysis.

32-a Finding a Subject to Write On

In searching for a topic for this kind of article, students can explore their own areas of expertise by looking in these places:

— employment background

— work done around the house

— volunteer work

— unusual experiences (climbing a mountain, digging for clams, dealing with injury/illness)

— travel

— sports one has played or otherwise knows a lot about

— hobbies (baseball card collecting, cooking)

— personal intellectual interests (history, poetry, theatre)

—subjects studied in school

   —experiences at school (preparing for the SAT, working on the yearbook).

Also, encourage students to explore subjects that they may have an interest in, but not a great deal of initial knowledge about. For example, a student may have wondered how tough Marine boot camp really is. Or how the Supreme Court decides whether or not to hear a case. If the assignment schedule gives students enough time, and it usually does, they can build up their expertise through research. Portfolio assessment allows them to continue adding information to their essay beyond the due dates for drafts.

32-b *Structure and Content for an Informative Essay*

The introduction of an informative essay or article is important. *English Journal*, an academic publication for high school teachers and others interested in secondary education, publishes this statement for those who would submit articles: "Beginning paragraphs should clearly indicate: what the manuscript addresses; why anyone should care to read it; and why the writer is qualified to speak on the subject."

You might ask your students to provide that kind of information in their introduction:

   —A clear statement of the topic

   —The importance of the topic (why the reader should be interested)

   —The writer's qualifications to talk about this subject.

Find or write a couple of examples, like this one:

32. The Informative Essay

SAMPLE INTRODUCTION

Rigging a sailboat refers to putting up the masts and sails and tying down the lines in preparation for sailing. It is important to rig a sailboat correctly; otherwise the boat will not move efficiently through the water. I learned this the hard way when I went beyond casual sailing and got involved in racing. This article will show you how rigging should be done on a small sailboat and what mistakes to avoid so as to always do it correctly.

Note that the introduction includes a definition (of rigging). The early paragraphs are a good place for defining important terms. For example, if the student is writing on the subject of campus date rape, it would be important to define *date rape* in detail at the outset. So to the list of what goes into an introduction, you could include important definitions. Some technical articles begin with a short glossary of terms used in the article. Some of your students, if writing on a highly technical subject, might like to begin their informative essay with a brief glossary of terms and definitions.

For the complete structure of an informative article, the introduction indicates the direction for the whole text, the body delivers on the promises in the introduction, and the conclusion takes one of the standard forms (like those listed in Section 30-e 8). You can have students produce the three parts separately for review, or altogether in a full draft. If you wanted groups to look at introductions, it would be easy to create a Critique Sheet for that purpose, such as:

Y/N The writer . . .

___ Clearly identifies the topic

___ Indicates the importance of the topic

___ Establishes the writer's expertise

___ Defines important terms

Below that would appear any Point To's you wanted to include in the Critique Sheet.

32-c *Audience Awareness and Analysis*

Technical writers distinguish between expert-to-expert and expert-to-novice texts, but compositions are always going to be expert-to-novice. The student knows about something, or knows how to do something, and he assumes that his audience is basically clueless. This is good because it teaches the need for audience awareness in writing.

Most first-year students do not have a sophisticated concept of audience. They assume that the only person who ever reads anything intellectual that they write is their teacher, who reads to correct, criticize, and grade—not to get useful information. In real life beyond the classroom, of course, writers never write for such an audience. And even in college, students will gradually start writing for imagined audiences broader than just their teacher.

It is useful to ask students to undertake a formal audience analysis before writing their informative essay. They can begin by answering questions like the ones below during the planning stage, and you can have them turn in their answers as a homework assignment:

—Who are my readers? Who would want to read this text?

—What do I want my readers to know about this subject?

—What do my readers already know? What will I have to tell them?

It is possible to invent homework or in-class exercises that help students understand the concept of audience. For example, you can have them write a set of directions to your office, first for someone who went to school here last semester,

32. The Informative Essay

and then again, this time for someone who has never been to the campus. They will soon realize that they will have to provide more information for the latter audience, and that's why audience consideration is important.

Here's another brief exercise along the same lines: Imagine you are living in an apartment off campus. Write a supermarket shopping list for yourself with at least ten items on it. [After your students have finished their list, give them this next writing task.] Now imagine that an emergency prevents you from doing the shopping, but a next door neighbor is going to the supermarket and volunteers to get the items. Rewrite the shopping list so that the neighbor gets the same items that you would have purchased. For example, instead of "peaches," write "canned peaches" or "fresh peaches."

After the two lists have been composed, ask students to share with the class differences that arose in their two lists.

32-d Writing Instructions

This assignment gives students a chance to do some very practical writing. Again, audience analysis is crucial. If some readers lack necessary background knowledge, they will not be able to understand and follow the instructions. The writer must consider such possible limitations on the part of the audience and address them.

In devising subjects to write on, students can draw on knowledge they brought with them to college and on information they have picked up on campus. For example:

—How to use a complicated piece of equipment in the workout gym

—How to find an article in the library

—How to use the photocopying machine in the library

—How to maintain the animal cages in the zoology lab

—How to create and maintain a herbal garden

—How to get high gas mileage out of your car

—How to tune a piano.

The classic assignment for instructional writing is a good one: "How to Fix a Flat Tire." In any composition class there will be one or more students whose friend or spouse or sweetie doesn't know how to do this with her own car (or *his* own car). The writer can figure out how to do it with that particular automobile and then write a useful set of instructions to be kept in the glove compartment. The writer can carry out a usability test by having the car owner try out the instructions, removing one of the good tires and replacing it with the spare tire.

Here are some things you can teach students about instructional writing:

1. Use an informative title, such as "How to Submit a Draft Composition through the Computer Network" or "How to Properly Make an Omelet."

2. Present preliminary information. Often a reader has to go to some location or gather certain equipment before starting the process being taught.

3. Present instructions in numbered steps.

4. Prominently place warnings where missteps could cause trouble.

5. Use visuals to clarify steps.

6. Perform a usability test. (A member of the imagined audience carries out the written instructions while the writer watches and notes any confusion or missteps.) Revise accordingly.

32. The Informative Essay

Technical writing textbooks, like Murdick and Bloemker's *The Portable Technical Writer,* and some composition textbooks, like Murdick's *A Student Guide to College Composition, 2nd Ed.*, provide detail about each of the six components listed above. On the basis of that kind of information, you can expand your lectures. You can also devise the worst instructions in the world, alongside excellent instructions, to use as examples for your class. In addition, it is easy to find real life examples of both good and bad instructions to use as illustrations. Just be on the lookout for them in your daily private and professional life. (They are all over campus, and in almost every office in administration buildings.) You can leave a collection of them on reserve in the library for student inspection and critique, or reproduce examples with permission of the copyright holder, if there is one. Government documents, such as the publications of state colleges and universities, are in the public domain and are not copyrighted. However, such documents may have privacy requirements which cannot be violated and they may quote copyrighted text, the writer having obtained permission for that document only (not yours). So be careful.

33

The Argument on a Controversial Issue

In this assignment, students learn about important philosophical, social, and political issues, including those that have been around in the West since the Golden Age of Greece and those making headlines today. You have several options as to what approaches to argumentation to teach and require. If the whole course centers on this kind of writing, you can introduce all of them.

Most textbooks in this genre focus on classical argumentation, the attempt to convince an audience of the correctness of your view, using methods introduced by Aristotle and formalized by Cicero. You might warn your students that such arguments rarely work. However, a writer can convince a skeptical or disbelieving reader that her view is grounded in good will, evidence, and reasoning. That's an achievement. And there is always the minority of readers who come to a text without a fixed opinion, and they can be persuaded.

The classical argument can be re-conceptualized as the presentation of a problem and its solution. And in particular, you might present cause-effect reasoning as being at the heart of problem-solution rhetoric. These ideas are discussed below.

Finally, you have the option of offering students the difficult task of producing a compromise argument in which the writer finds similarities in two opposing sides and forges a compromise that attempts to satisfy the strongest concerns of both.

33. The Argument on a Controversial Issue

33-a Classical Argumentation Structure

It is useful, in the first assignment for a particular category of essay, that you present students with a simplified structure, at least for their first drafts. This introduces them to the elements that have to be present in such an essay. For a classical argument, you might offer this structure:

— Identification of the issue and perhaps why it is controversial
— Presentation of the opposing view
— Concession to that view
— Rebuttal of that view
— Presentation of the writer's view
— Defense of that view

If you are using a textbook reader containing arguments on controversial issues, you will be able to reveal, or allow the students to find, examples of these elements in essays during class discussion. The local daily newspapers and even the campus student newspaper will provide other examples of argumentation texts. In addition, many argumentation essays can be found on the Web, where your students can read them and even print them out (such material is in the public domain). For example, this book uses Michael Levin's essay "The Case for Torture" as an example on a couple of occasions. At the time of this writing, that essay is available at **http://people.brandeis.edu/~teuber/torture.html**, among other locations.

It is useful to introduce students to the language of argumentation. For example, when discussing the presentation of the opponents' views, you can provide them with a list of formulaic phrases like these (from Murdick's *A Student Guide to College Composition, 2n Ed.*):

— Those who support X argue that . . .

— Those who oppose X point out that . . .

— Those who argue that X . . .

— Those who defend the view that X . . .

— Opponents of X often point out that . . .

— Advocates of X say that . . .

— Those who advocate X believe that. . . .

It is useful to introduce students to some basics of logic and reasoning, such as how to avoid (or attack in the writing of opponents) a straw man argument, a false premise, a false analogy, an over-generalization, etc. If you need to deepen your own understanding of these aspects of reasoning, many rhetoric textbooks take them up in detail, including those by the author of this book (see *Writing and Reasoning* and *A Student Guide to College Composition, 2nd Ed.*).

33-b Problem-Solution Argumentation

Here is a simplified structure you can require or recommend for your students for their first draft:

— Statement of a problem
— False solutions that have been proposed or tried out, or that the reader might think of
— Why those solutions won't work
— Your solution
— Why your solution will work.

Point out to your students that in this kind of essay the writer might emphasize the nature of the problem, since once that is determined, the solution may become obvious.

For example, are weak public schools, where they exist, the result of under-funding, poor teaching, or a bad curriculum? In each of those cases, certain solutions are obvious, once the problem has been determined. If under-funding is the problem, then more funding will solve it; if poor teaching is the problem, then better teacher training is called for; if the curriculum is bad, then it must be changed.

In other cases, most people may agree on the problem, but different groups offer different solutions. If writing on the drug problem in the U.S., for example, one could do so by looking mainly at the different solutions that have been proposed, saying little about the problem itself. Other topics call for a more balanced discussion of problem and solution. Ask your students to analyze the social problem they are writing about, to determine where the focus ought to be.

33-c *Cause-Effect Reasoning*

As with problem-solution reasoning, cause-effect discussions require an analysis to determine whether the causes or the effects, or both, should be the focus of the essay. Let's first look at the option of writing about what causes something bad or something good. Suppose, for example, that the high school students at a school are doing poorly on standardized tests. One can argue about what the cause of this low performance might be: the culture of poverty from which the students come, student laziness, poor teaching, a bad curriculum, insufficient funding of the school by the state government. All of those are possible causes; any of them might produce the particular known effect—the low test scores. Which one is the true cause? That could be the subject of a persuasive cause-effect essay.

But here is another complication to the example of low test scores. All of the causes mentioned may play a role in producing that effect. The question then is: Which one is the *main* cause? This is a very practical question, because the time, energy, personnel, and money available to solve social problems is always limited. We normally want to focus on the main causes of a problem first, but to do that we have to identify them, distinguishing them from less important (though real) causes. The same would be true if the student were writing on the possible causes of one high school's high test scores.

Alternatively, your composition students may want to focus on effects. Here is a passage in which the effects are the focus:

> While many politicians and some educators believe that standardized tests are agents of change in the right direction in our schools today, such tests can have negative effects as well. High stakes testing, in which schools are judged by the scores that their students make, has resulted, in many cases, in a narrowing of the curriculum to test preparation. In such an environment, students engage in subjects to a shallower degree, as they focus only on those items that can be tested through multiple choice questions. That means abandoning rich educational experiences, such as research report writing and group projects.
>
> In addition, the tests have created a new category of student failure: the "push out." Push outs are weak students who drop out of school because their teachers and administrators encourage them to. The school officials are worried that the students' low test scores will hurt the school average. Students who don't finish high school in our society are likely headed for a life of minimum-wage poverty or crime.

The possible effects of a policy or action are often the subject of debate. If we raise teachers' salaries, will that result in more accomplished people entering the teaching profession, or will it merely result in teachers taking more expensive vacations? Writers may also disagree about the effects of something that has already happened. Have increases in school funding, where such increases have occurred, improved education in those schools? That could be a matter of debate because it is not always clear how to recognize or measure such improvement.

33-d Pitfalls in Cause-Effect Reasoning

Cause-effect argumentation obviously provides good writing challenges for composition students. But before assigning such a paper, it would be wise to alert them to certain problems that can arise in this kind of reasoning.

Writers sometimes mistakenly assume that because one thing happened earlier than another, the first event *caused* the later event, or a policy that was initiated earlier than an effect caused that effect. In reality the first event may not have caused, or may not have been the only cause, of the event. Medical science is plagued by this problem. You get ill, you take a pill, the illness goes away. You therefore assume that the pill caused the illness to retreat. But medical scientists know that almost all ailments go away on their own after a period of time, even if nothing is done to treat them. The medical treatment may have helped, it may have sped up recovery, but it may not have. So medical researchers have to use elaborate methods of testing treatments. To test a new drug, for example, they might compare the recovery history of an experimental group, who take the medicine, with that of control groups, one of which takes a placebo (a fake drug or "sugar pill") and one of which undergoes no treatment at all. Only after careful studies of this sort have consistently shown the experimental group doing better than the control groups would the researchers conclude that the drug has a healthful effect.

Writers often mistake correlation for cause-effect. Suppose in your home town in recent years the number of churches has increased and so has the number of bars. Does this mean that religion drives people to drink? In other words, is religion the cause of the need for more bars? Or does drink create sinners, who are then drawn to churches? Probably neither. Both increases are almost certainly the effect of another, not-yet-mentioned cause, such as an increase in the town's population.

Most policies have both good and bad effects. It isn't just one or the other. Suppose, for example, that the student writer supports the legalization of marijuana and presents various reasons why that would be a good idea—various good effects of legalization. A reader may be wondering all the while: What about the obvious bad effects? Marijuana impairs depth perception, for example, making driving under its influence potentially dangerous. If the student writer doesn't recognize such problems and come up with answers to them in his essay, the reader may find his reasoning unconvincing. In such a situation, weighing the good against the bad will become the central argument of the essay.

Alert your students to the fact that some cause-effect phenomena are best understood as sequences of cause-effect. In one professional study, for example, the researchers, after looking at data on car accident injuries, noted that smokers suffer more injuries during accidents than non-smokers. It seemed that smoking somehow caused more injuries. But how could that be? Further research showed that smokers, seeking more mobility to carry out the motions of getting and lighting cigarettes and using ashtrays, were more likely to leave seat belts unbuckled. Clearly, the direct cause of the difference in injuries was the difference in seat belt use. Still, smoking was the original, indirect cause.

Such cause-effect situations have to be understood as a sequence or chain of causes and effects: **cause→effect/ cause→effect**. In the case of smoking and injuries, a writer could not come up with a solution to the problem of more injuries until she understood the sequence that leads to them. Without understanding that sequence, she might suggest that people stop smoking when driving (advice that probably won't be taken by many). However, if she understands the sequence, she might more profitably suggest a law

33. The Argument on a Controversial Issue

requiring seatbelts that automatically engage and disengage with the opening and closing of the car door.

33-e Compromise Argument

To figure out a compromise solution, the student has to look at the issue from the perspective of one group and then the other. What does each side really, ultimately want—institutional improvement, peace, fairness, redress of past wrongs, respect, authority? Often they both want the same thing, the same outcome. Or if they want different things, they may not necessarily conflict. And often the way to get there is through a recognition of the legitimate concerns of each side, as well as a sense of what each side will have to give up.

Most of your composition students will be struggling with the task of arguing one side of an argument, but the compromise argument can make a good assignment if they reach a point where they seem to have gotten a handle on classic argumentation. As a teacher, you will often have to make judgments about how much to challenge your students. If they are not trying to do something beyond their abilities, they are not learning. But if the challenge is too great, their efforts may yield only confusion and frustration.

34

The Literary Criticism Essay

Professional critics approach a piece of literature knowing all of the author's works, knowing where the author fits into the history of literature, knowing how the author imitates and differs from her contemporaries, knowing what creative writers have done and what they generally do in various genres (short story, poem, novel, play), and knowing formal critical perspectives that can be utilized in their analysis. Your composition students know none of that. Obviously, whatever your students do in the way of literary criticism, it is not going to be what critics are doing in the literary journals.

This should not prevent your students, however, from finding beauty and meaning in a piece of literature, and then writing about it.

34-a *Personal and Community Meaning*

Scholars looking into the nature of reading have made a useful discovery: No two people can possibly read the same complex text, such as a piece of literature, precisely the same way. Reading ultimately consists of creating a text in your mind through contact with a written work. However, the particular mental text that you create will be strongly affected by conditions outside the written text itself, the three most important being (1) your purpose in reading, (2) your prior personal experience with the subject matter of the written text, and (3) your culture and era.

34. The Literary Criticism Essay

Purpose is easy to understand. As one experiment showed, groups of people reading a description of a house remembered different details of the text according to whether they were told to read it as potential home buyers or professional thieves. As for personal experience, suppose we are reading a paragraph which says that a cat suddenly appears around the side of a couch and walks across the room, and that paragraph provides no details about the cat. Everyone brings different experiences with cats to such a reading. Some of us might see a white cat moving gracefully, others a gray cat moving stealthily, and others an orange cat hopping playfully. Yet we are all reading the same text.

But that's not the whole story. Most of us read the cat passage in very similar ways, as well. We all have about the same sense of what a cat is. Because we are Americans in the 21st c., we imagine a house cat, not a lion or a tiger. The word *couch* evokes in our minds similar images. And what happened in the scene was the same for all of us. We read the passage alike, quite simply, because we belong to the same culture in the same era.

The cat story shows us that we can find both personal and community meaning in a literary text. In asking your students to interpret a piece of literature, start with the personal, and then segue to the community. Ask your students first: How is this text meaningful to you? Then ask them: What meaning does this text hold for your friends, family, and community?

Here are some cues to making personal meaning out of a piece of literature that you can offer your students as starting points:

>—The pleasure the language affords you, your enjoyment of the interesting or attractive sounds coming from the text, your delight in the beautiful phrasing. In poetry especially, the sound of a poem can affect your mood or contribute to some of the effect. Always

read a poem aloud a couple of times, as well as silently. What is the sound communicating to you?

—Your reaction to the narrator. If the poem or story has a narrator, a fictional person speaking the poem or telling the story, listen for the tone of that person's voice and consider how that speaker strikes you—is the speaker a delicate lady, a cool dude, a con man? Do you like or dislike the narrator as a person? Do you trust what the narrator says? Who does the narrator remind you of in your personal life?

—The evocation of a memory of some event that was important in your life, perhaps an event that shaped who you are, or made you realize something. Now you are being reminded of the event in circumstances that allow you to reconsider it.

—The recognition of yourself being described, providing a clearer understanding of who you are.

—The recognition of a type of familiar person being described, deepening your understanding of that person, or type of person, perhaps someone important to you such as a parent or friend, or a type of person you know from your circle of friends, such as a daredevil or an ambitious person.

—The recognition of a place, or type of place, which is a part of your life, perhaps evoking a set of memories. Such descriptions renew and sharpen your sense of this place—why is it important to you? What details in the piece of literature bring back the memory?

—The recognition of a smell—autumn leaves burning, the heavy heat of a locker room, your mother's perfume—so that you relive an episode or a time in your life, regaining those memories. This may lead to a comparison of then and now. Not only smell but other senses—visual images, the feel or taste of something—can stir up memories and ideas

—The evocation of a feeling: a sense of regret that you once felt, or the elation over some accomplishment, or the nervous ecstasy of love, suddenly coming over you as though you were going through that experience again—what do you know now that you didn't know then?

—The recognition of a story line, of how human character leads you, or others you know, on a familiar course to a foreseeable end; an understanding of why things happened as they did in your life.

And then the extension of these evocations to the community:

—The recognition of not just yourself and individuals you know, but of a community, such as Catholic high school students, the Bronx's Asian community, the oystermen of the Florida panhandle, the elderly living their last months in an institution. Or even the recognition of your country as a community, perhaps a sense of national destiny.

—A recognition of our humanity, our similarity with others, and from that a new understanding of what it means to be human.

—Our place in the universe, perhaps alone and insignificant, perhaps integrated and important.

You will need to model personal criticism, using perhaps a poem you like. What is it about this poem that you like? Communicate that to your students. Let them see how literature affects people, how it can affect them if they open themselves up to it.

Here is a model response from a student to this Shakespearian sonnet:

> My mistress' eyes are nothing like the sun;
>   Coral is far more red, than her lips red:
>   If snow be white, why then her breasts are dun;
>   If hairs be wires, black wires grow on her head.
>   I have seen roses damask'd, red and white,
>   But no such roses see I in her cheeks;
>   And in some perfumes is there more delight
>   Than in the breath that from my mistress reeks.
>   I love to hear her speak, yet well I know
>   That music hath a far more pleasing sound:
>   I grant I never saw a goddess go,—
> My mistress, when she walks, treads on the ground:
>   And yet by heaven, I think my love as rare,
>   As any she belied with false compare.

1st Draft of a Personal Response:

In Sonnet 131, Shakespeare is making fun of poets who say glorious things about their true love, comparing her to beautiful things. Things that are a lot more beautiful than she really is. Nobody has breath as nice as perfume. It sounds like the narrator is criticizing his girlfriend by saying that she can't compare to roses and she walks along the ground instead of floating like a goddess. But then he pulls a switcheroo, saying at the end that he really loves her, and you believe him because he hasn't been a phony all along, saying false things about her. He's been honest, so he has credibility when he finally says he loves her.

In real life you have to love people who are imperfect. My fiancée is a handsome guy, but he's short, just barely taller

34. The Literary Criticism Essay

than me. He gets OK grades, but he isn't super-smart. He's not going to invent the next million-dollar money maker. But he's not a phony and he's the one I want to be with. "I think my love as rare," as the narrator says, as any guy around. I'm sure he thinks I'm imperfect, too, but that's OK because I know he really loves me.

If you wanted to get this student to start developing a community response, you might ask her to think about the credibility issue that she touched on in the first paragraph. How can that be expanded beyond the realm of love talk?

34-b Conventions of Writing Criticism

Professional writers have ready-made sentence constructions in their mental "object libraries" which allow them to write quickly and smoothly even in complex situations. For instance, they have ways of introducing a piece of writing and its author, and this is something useful that you can teach your students. Show them patterns that work and those that don't. A writer has the option of making either the author or the title the subject of the sentence:

Possibility #1: Make the author the subject of the sentence

a) Emily Dickenson, in her poem "In Winter in My Room," describes a nightmare in which a worm turns into a sensuous snake and threatens a young girl.

b) In her poem "In Winter in My Room," Emily Dickenson describes a nightmare in which a worm turns into a sensuous snake and threatens a young girl.

Possibility #2: Make the title the subject of the sentence

c) "In Winter in My Room," by Emily Dickenson, describes a nightmare in which a worm turns into a sensuous snake and threatens a young girl.

d) Emily Dickenson's "In Winter in My Room" describes a nightmare in which a worm turns into a sensuous snake and threatens a young girl.

DO NOT USE A PRONOUN AS THE SUBJECT

Wrong:

e) In the poem "In Winter in My Room," by Emily Dickenson, she describes a nightmare in which a worm turns into a sensuous snake and threatens a young girl.

f) In Emily Dickenson's "In Winter in My Room," she describes a nightmare in which a worm turns into a sensuous snake and threatens a young girl.

g) In the poem "In Winter in My Room," by Emily Dickenson, it describes a nightmare in which a worm turns into a sensuous snake and threatens a young girl.

Students must be taught to continually refer to, and quote from, the text that they are critiquing as they develop their view. These references and quotations are essential to giving credibility to the writer's arguments. Your students will not know this if you don't tell them and show them how. Create examples by critiquing a poem or short story yourself.

Below is an example of a student's community-meaning interpretation of Robert Francis's short poem "The Hound" (this example comes from *A Student Guide to College Composition, 2nd Ed.*). Using such an example in class, you would point out every place where the writer keeps her text connected to the piece of literature she is critiquing (those are printed in bold in the sample). In further examples, you would ask students to find the connections.

Limitations of Francis's "The Hound"

by Louise Gordon

In his poem "The Hound," Robert Francis uses a dog approaching at a run to represent uncertainty in life. Will the dog lick me or bite me? Will I live a good life, or a tormented one? This is a reasonable question, since we can look around us and see people who have everything, including happiness and a long life, and we can see people who have nothing, who are miserable and die young.

According to Francis, we cannot know what our fate will be: "I cannot tell / The hound's intent / Till he has sprung / At my bare hand / With teeth or tongue." We are in the dark. And this is true to some extent. A person's fate can change at any moment. Today you are rich and happy, tomorrow the stock market crashes or someone slips on your front steps and you are sued and end up in debt and miserable. Or one day a lover abandons you and you are miserable; but in the end you find someone else who is much better for you. We cannot predict what will happen to us.

Yet I am unsatisfied with this poem. It doesn't tell the whole story. **The poem's narrator is too passive: "Meanwhile I stand / And wait the event." He is too vulnerable: the hound leaps "At my bare hand."** Aren't there things that we can do to take control of our own lives? Can't we learn from experience? For example, a woman who has had only abusive relationships with men recently, as she begins to get involved again with a new man, must feel like **the narrator watching the approaching hound**. But she doesn't have to passively wait to see what happens. She can seek men who are not likely to be abusive. She can test the men she goes out with. She can make it clear to these men what she will not put up with. She need not **"stand and wait the event."**

Finally, your students need to be taught conventions of style for literary criticism. For example, in the first reference to an author, teach them to include the author's first and last names, but thereafter only the last name. Warn your students not to refer to authors by their first names alone:

> **Wrong:** Ernest does a good job of depicting post-war malaise in "A Soldier's Home."

> **Right:** Hemingway does a good job of depicting post-war malaise in "A Soldier's Home."

Teach your students to use the present tense, to write "the hound races toward the narrator," not "the hound raced toward the narrator," and "Francis has his narrator stand passively instead of resisting," not "Francis had his narrator stand passively instead of resisting."

34-d *The Character Study*

Literature, of course, is more than something of personal meaning to a particular reader. There is an art to it. Part of that art lies in the beautiful writing, part in the development of themes or ideas. The latter are part of the writer's intentions, not the reader's, and readers need be alert to them in order to appreciate the work fully. In other words, the reader is not the only meaning maker. The writer creates a meaning meant to be shared by all readers.

When professional critics write about literature as art, they try to show the methods by which the author or the work creates meaning. When talking about meaning in this sense, we can use the term "theme." Literary works have "themes"; that is, they develop major ideas, some of which are quite standard and reappear in many works: loss of innocence, loss of faith, maturation, corruption of society, good versus evil, the ugliness of war, the beauty of love, the meaninglessness

34. The Literary Criticism Essay

of life, the necessity of freedom, the interdependence of people. Note that these themes may contradict one another. Different writers view the world differently.

If you were to write an essay about a piece of literature as a work of art, you might trace how the setting, or certain images, or the symbols the author has created contribute to the development of the themes of the work. To do so in depth requires a substantial introduction to literary criticism, including some technical terminology. Some colleges do offer a first-year course which combines composition and the study of literature, but most don't.

One way to get around your students' lack of professional training in literary criticism is ask them to write a character study using a short story or a play or a long poem (they probably won't have time to read a novel). This they can do with no training, relying simply on their own experiences in life. Thousands of years ago, the Greek philosopher Heraclitus stated that "A man's character is his fate." In other words, the kind of person you are determines what happens to you in life and how you affect others. The purpose of a character study is to prove Heraclitus right in regard to a fictional character.

Another important feature of fiction is the existence of conflict or trial. It is out of such struggles that a character's true character comes to life and determines or affects the outcome. For instance, the main character in Jack London's "To Build a Fire" is up against a harsh nature in the arctic, and he is probably doomed from the start in that contest, regardless of who he is, but it is his character that assures his demise and which got him into his predicament in the first place. That is the sort of thing you want your students to come to understand and reveal in their essays.

Point out that characters may be in conflict with themselves; that is, with their dual natures or conflicting desires. Or, as in the case of Jack London's protagonist, with nature. Or with God or some other element of the supernatural (Amanda Hocking's wildly popular teenage vampire novels illustrate the latter theme). The character your student is writing about may be in conflict with another character or a group or a community. Moliere's protagonist in *Le Misanthrope* is at odds with humanity.

The purpose of the student's paper is to describe the fictional character's nature and personality and then the conflict the character is caught up in (this is not a beginning-to-end plot summary, but a focused analysis). Finally, the paper should show how the character's nature contributes to the outcome of the conflict. Provide your students with an example, one in which you provide an interpretation of a literary character.

You have to make sure that your students are writing on a piece of literature or choosing from list of works that you yourself are familiar with so you can judge their interpretations and help them along. If your textbook contains several short works, you're OK. Otherwise, create a list for them to choose from, using works in the public domain. They are easy to find. For example, this site has the full text of about twenty short stories by famous writers:

http://www.rainsnow.org/cshf_public_domain_stories.htm

You might choose four of these stories, and then each student would select a character from one of them. Point out that the main character or protagonist is the most obvious target for description, and probably the easiest to write about, but that the second-most-important character often makes an interesting object of study.

35

The Long Research Paper

For our purposes here, we will assume that a long research paper runs about ten double-spaced manuscript pages and has a bibliography with about ten entries. Even in first-year composition, such papers may end up substantially longer, especially if a student becomes intensely interested in his subject.

35-a Your Preparation

If this is your first time to teach a writing course in which students have to produce a 10-page paper with 10 or more bibliographical sources, then you have much preparation to do. To begin, ask your composition director, or ask around among your colleagues, if they have any sample student research papers that you can look at to see what will be coming at you at the end of the semester. If they do, the texts will probably be A papers, which is what you want. Ask if the student writers have given permission for their papers to be used as examples, so that you can photocopy them and leave them on reserve in the library for your own students to examine.

If you are fortunate enough to get such samples, you might add to them a note addressed to your students indicating what qualities they should look for as they read these papers. It is easier to produce a new kind of text successfully if one has a good mental image of what the final product is supposed to look like. With such model papers and a short guide from you, your students won't be operating in the dark, always wondering if they are on the right track.

Your next major task is to learn your local campus library. Ask a research librarian to give you a tour, essentially the same one she (or you) will give your students just before they start their research project. You should make sure that your students get a tour, even if they already had one as part of an earlier composition course. This time it will really mean something to them, since so much of their course work will be focused on this project. Besides the book stacks and the references books, you and your students need to know where newspapers, magazines, journals, and every other type of periodical can be found and what online databases the library subscribes to. Also, teach your students how to use the library's photocopying machine and how to save online entries in the library database to their (the students') campus computer account or their e-mail address.

35-b *Helping Students Find Subjects to Write On*

Your students cannot get started on this long project until they have found a suitable subject to research and write on, and helping them do so won't be easy. Many students will struggle to find a do-able topic and some may end up producing a poor paper because their topic was never really suitable.

The essential problem is to find a subject that is not-too-big and not-too-small. If the subject is too big, the student's coverage will necessarily be shallow or unfocused. If it is too small, the student will not be able to find enough information to produce a 10-page text with a 10-entry bibliography. Provide your students with examples of both kinds of unworkable topics to illustrate this point. You might list pairs like this:

35. The Long Research Paper

TOO BIG: What's Wrong with our Economy (whole books have been written on this subject)

TOO SMALL: Why There Were No Jobs Programs in the Last Year of the Bush Administration (hard to find information on why something didn't happen; there may not even be any solid reasons for this, since big projects are rarely started in the last year of an administration)

TOO BIG: Are rock stars a good influence on teenagers? Too many rock stars, too many teenagers.

TOO SMALL: Is Lady Gaga changing minds about gay rights? This might work as one section on Lady Gaga's cultural influence, which would be a more suitable topic.

At the same time, by way of illustration, list some topics that have worked well. If this is your first term and you don't have any examples, ask some colleagues who have taught this course before to give you some titles that they thought produced good papers.

You can allow students to write on purely informative topics, though this may prove more difficult for them. Every topic has controversial elements, once you get into the details, and it is hard to avoid them. Here are some examples of topics that are largely informative:

— What was veterinary treatment like 100 years ago, compared to today?

— How have the methods and equipment of snipers changed over the centuries?

— What elements of the earliest stage designs (ancient Greek, Elizabethan, etc.) are still found in many modern productions?

Make sure that students understand that they can write on topics that they know almost nothing about but would like to learn about.

Students will not have much trouble finding persuasive topics to write on. A search of the Web for lists of such topics will provide ideas. So will any newspaper editorial page. Again, there are easily found Web sites with lists of topics, such as:

> https://www.kibin.com/essay-writing-blog/
> 20-persuasive-essay-topics-help-get-started/

Strongly suggest to students that they write on topics that interest them, on issues that fire them up. This is a long haul and writing on a boring topic can result in deadly procrastination.

In terms of conceptualization of a topic, one straightforward approach is for the students to raise a question that the essay will answer. For example, Is home schooling really a good idea? Or, How does peacetime service differ in the different branches of the military? In your first effort at teaching this assignment, you might require a thesis question.

35-c An Initial Bibliography

Once a student has an approved topic, he must determine whether he can find enough information on it from available resources, such as the campus library, the Web, and persons available to interview. So that is your next assignment for your students: Create an initial working bibliography. Once this project is underway, you need to monitor students' progress closely, helping those who need help finding sources or adjusting their topic. The sooner a student and you discover that a topic is a dead end, the sooner you can help the student get started on a more productive inquiry.

At this point, you should introduce students to the formatting of bibliographical entries. Show them (1) the several kinds they are most likely to use, such as books and Web articles, and (2) how to use their handbook to handle other types of sources. This calls for a lecture-practice-quiz approach. Don't ask students to memorize many different bibliographic formats; they will just forget them after your quiz. But do insist that they learn how to use their handbook to obtain the correct format for various sources. This can be done through class work and homework.

35-d Creation of a Tentative Outline

Students need to first acquire some general knowledge of their subject by reading the most general sources in their working bibliography. Wikipedia is a good place to start. The purpose of acquiring general knowledge is to be able to create a tentative outline in preparation for further reading, research, and note taking.

An outline here means a set of section titles which break up the topic into the parts that will be developed. Say the student is writing on the issue of legalizing marijuana. After some initial general reading, he might produce an outline like the one below, reflecting his new knowledge of the issue:

I. Definition and description of marijuana

II. Dangerous chemical effects of marijuana

III. Beneficial chemical effects of (medical) marijuana

IV. A brief history of marijuana laws in the U.S.

V. The bad effects of criminalization on the justice system

VI. Will decriminalization work?

It is very important that your students put together such an outline as soon as possible so that they can select items to read and can determine what notes to take. Without such an outline, they cannot judge whether it is worth their time to read a particular text. Nor can they determine what information and quotations they should extract and put in their collection of notes.

35-e *Note Taking*

Show your students a system by which they number each note with a Roman numeral that will connect the note to a section of their paper (each section having its own Roman numeral, as in the marijuana example above). Teach them to add another code to each note that will connect the note to an entry in the working bibliography, perhaps the author's initials or last name followed by the first three words of the title.

Encourage a habit of making the bibliographical entry before doing any note taking. Or, when that's not convenient, teach your students to extract sufficient information to later make the bibliographical entry, such as title, author, volume, publisher, date of publication, date of accessing a Web site, page numbers, etc. You might have them create a sheet listing required information for various kinds of sources, a sheet that they can carry with them and consult whenever they are in the library or otherwise away from their personal computer and doing research.

Too often students end up with a beautiful quotation or an important note which they cannot use because they don't have the full bibliographical information and cannot relocate the source or can't find the page numbers within a source.

Notes can be taken on the traditional 3 X 5 cards, though nowadays the omnipresence of copying machines and computers makes the use of full sheets of paper a convenient approach. The student can photocopy a page of text, and then use a pen to mark the relevant sentences and to put the Roman numeral and bibliography code at the top of the page. He can also make marginal notes with his pen, putting down his thoughts about how the marked information or idea will contribute to his line of reasoning in this section of his text.

35. The Long Research Paper

If a page has content pertinent to two different sections, it would be photocopied twice, so that a copy can go in each of two piles of notes.

One advantage of the photocopied full page method of note taking is that there is never any confusion as to the language the original author used, which helps with the plagiarism problem and makes quoting easy. Also, the page numbers should appear on the photocopied page, so they can't be accidentally neglected or lost.

Web articles, of course, would be printed in whole or part, not photographed. Tell students to record the date they accessed Web articles because that won't show up even if they print the whole article.

As the process proceeds, the student sorts the notes into different piles, one pile for each Roman numeral. At the end of the research process, the student takes each of the piles separately, orders the notes, and then writes it up as a section of his text. This turns the writing of a 10-page paper into the writing of three or four papers that are two to four pages in length, something first-year students can handle.

35-f Let the Writing Begin

Once your students have done most of their reading and note-taking, they are ready to start writing up the sections. Of course, they may discover as they write that they need more information. The process of creating a research paper isn't purely linear; it is going to be somewhat recursive.

Before they start the actual writing, you might run them through these in-class exercises:

(1) Ask them to write a couple of paragraphs providing an introduction to their paper. The introduction should reveal the nature of the topic, its importance, and the direction(s) the writer is going to develop it.

(2) Ask them to write a summary of their whole paper before they write up the first section. This puts an overview in their heads, which will guide them as they write up the individual sections.

Eventually you will want to review the first actual section, Roman numeral I. You might have student groups do an analysis of this section in class, on the class meeting before the section is turned in to you, so that writers can make some adjustments before you receive the text. To the normal Critique Sheet, you can add critical points like these:

___ Y ___ N   The section seems like an appropriate beginning

___ Y ___ N   The section seems to be fully developed

___ Y ___ N   I understood everything in this section

___ Y ___ N   The parenthetical notes are done correctly

___ Y ___ N   Quotations are handled correctly

Ask students to submit to you a copy of their whole outline along with the first section. You will keep the outline in an individual manila folder for each student. At the end of the term, you can ask each student to turn in all his notes along with the final copy of his paper. Pass out the manila folders in class so the students can put their collection of notes and drafts in them, the final copy on top. Any quizzes, homework, and critiqued drafts can be placed on top of the final copy in the order you indicate in your grading sheet, which would go on top of everything in the folder.

If the students know that they will have to turn in all their notes and drafts at the end of the term, some of it with your comments on it, they will think twice about trying to cheat by downloading a paper from the Internet.

35. The Long Research Paper

35-g Using Office Meetings

There is no way to keep on top of students' efforts without meeting with them in person. In those meetings the students will talk to you about their developing knowledge of their subject, and you will critique their work in progress.

Do not hesitate to cancel classes to make way for such meetings in your office. Find things for your students to do related to their developing essays in place of attending a class, such as interviewing someone or adding several new sources to their working bibliography. Be sure to warn your composition director or department chair that you are going to do this, making a note of your conversation in your CYA notebook. Administrators high up in the bureaucracy may not appreciate or understand pedagogies that include class cancellations, and if one of them hears that you are not meeting your students in the classroom, she may get upset and call you in for a meeting. If you have the OK from your immediate boss, as well as a clear, prepared explanation, there should be no problem. Bring this book to the meeting and read this paragraph aloud, if you wish. Show & tell. You are following the advice of a published, professional guide.

In short, the rationale is that meetings are necessary (1) to keep students on track and prevent anyone from falling hopelessly behind, and (2) to prevent plagiarism and cheating.

35-h Organizing Office Meetings

If you have an office mate, warn her that the mob is coming. If this creates a problem, find an empty office somewhere else on campus. The library often has meeting rooms available.

Once you have your students' first sections in hand, pass around a sign-up sheet for individual meetings. The sheet should list days and times when you will be in your office.

Allow each student at least ten minutes. Urge them to contact you as soon as possible if they are going to miss a meeting, so you can reschedule it. Attendance at each meeting might count a couple of points in the portfolio grade, but only one point for a re-scheduled meeting.

If a student has not turned in a first section for you to evaluate and has not scheduled a meeting, it should be clear that he is not on track to produce a long research paper. It is essential that you contact that student via e-mail, or talk to him after class if he is showing up, and demand a meeting within a week. Make a note of the name of the student in your CYA notebook and start keeping track of his non-progress. He may become a problem at final grade time, especially if he turns in a polished research paper you knew nothing about, a paper that was almost certainly written by someone else.

Make it clear to your students at the outset that you will not accept a paper if you have not been meeting with the student and have not had an opportunity to review drafts from the paper as the term progressed. Put that in your syllabus and announce it in class more than once. Make a note in your CYA notebook of the dates when you made such announcements.

35-i *Plagiarism and Cheating*

If you are monitoring your students' work, plagiarism should not be a problem, or at least not a problem that you can't nip in the bud before it ends up in the final version. During each meeting in your office, point out any phrasing you suspect is not theirs. Remind them to use quotation marks whenever they are borrowing phrasing. If you keep doing this in meetings, they will learn that they are not going to get away with plagiarism on the sentence level, and they will stop doing it.

As students submit sections and you get to see their notes, you should be able to tell if there are direct connections between notes and text. In other words, it will be very difficult, if not impossible, for any student to be using a borrowed or purchased paper (which would come *without* notes). You can also ask your students to discuss sections in their outline that they haven't written up yet. If they are doing their own work, they should be authorities on those sub-topics once they have done the reading and note taking, even if they haven't written anything yet.

Make it clear to your students at the outset that you will be following the above procedure, to head off any thoughts about cheating whole scale. Fraternities and sororities keep research papers in files, and professional essay-writing businesses advertise on the Web. Make it easier for your students to do their own work than to borrow or buy a paper and fake it through several meetings with you and several drafts that would have to be revised.

As indicated earlier, your policy should be that you will not read, nor accept, a research paper that you haven't seen during its development. Students cannot simply turn in a paper at the end of the term and get credit for it.

35-j Grading the Long Paper

The grade students earn on this assignment will probably count for at least half of their grade in the course, so you owe it to them to approach the task in a planned, intelligent way. And it is only fair to students that they know the criteria that you will be using to evaluate their work. You should be using an analytical scale instead of grading holistically for this assignment (see 26-b).

Figure 5 provides a model assessment scale. The number of points the student receives for each of the eight criteria below would be hand written into the blanks to the left of each statement. The highest possible number of points that can be earned appears in parentheses at the end of the statement.

Give your scale to your students at the outset of the project.

Figure 5: Model Assessment Scale for the Long Research Paper

1) ___ pts. Attended three meetings (6 pts)

2) ___ pts. The paper was turned in on time (4 pts)

3) ___ pts. The essay is of adequate length and is based on an adequate number of sources (5 pts)

4) ___ pts. The writer's purpose of being informative or presenting an argument is achieved successfully (35 pts)

5) ___ pts. The writer's voice dominates (10 pts)

6) ___ pts. Summaries, paraphrases, and quotations are appropriately and smoothly incorporated into the text (15 pts)

7) ___ pts. The essay is well edited and proofread (10 pts)

8) ___ pts. In-text parenthetical notes are done correctly (10 pts)

9) ___ pts. The bibliography is done correctly (10 pts)

Using high school math, you can figure out how many points to give a student for a B grade on, let's say, criterion #4. That would be 85 percent of 35, or 30 pts.

Afterword:
Becoming a Great Teacher

You will not start out your career as a great teacher. You may start out as a competent one, if you have natural talent and some good guidance. But greatness in this profession comes with experience, with learning how to handle the array of unplanned situations that arise in your courses and classrooms, with learning how students think and feel and learn, with learning what methods work best for you, and with learning what you can accomplish and what you should want to accomplish. That takes time. Years.

You can help the process along by being active in your professional discipline. That means reading the journals and important books; belonging to professional organizations; attending conferences; conducting research that tests your own ideas; writing articles, even if they don't get published; and arranging for serious student evaluations at the end of each term.

It can also mean meeting with a few colleagues on a Friday afternoon at a local tavern to complain about students and administrators over a cold one—and to pass on ideas for the classroom. It helps to have friends who are engaged in the same professional work and share your aspirations. To an important degree, writing, teaching, and learning are all social activities, as your own methods in the classroom and your own experience there should confirm.

Printed in the United States
By Bookmasters